THE MIDDLE EAST

Its Religion and Culture

THE MIDDLE EAST

Its Religion and Culture

by

EDWARD J. JURJI

Philadelphia

THE WESTMINSTER PRESS

Library of Congress Catalog Card Number: 56–9553

PRINTED IN THE UNITED STATES OF AMERICA

CONTENTS

FOREWORD

TEETERING between war and peace, the Middle East has captured the headlines and held world attention. Its role in religion has dwindled, however; and its stature in culture has receded. Modern man evidently has cared little how the moral factors in the Middle East situation have added up. His avowed ambition apparently has been economic, to insure an increasingly finer standard of living. A grim note in his daily life obviously has been psychological, an anxiety as the specter of total extinction loomed. Measured against concerns such as these, the issues posed in this book do at first seem remote.

Yet, what the book tries to say is peculiarly relevant. It runs close to everyone's heartbeat, for it touches upon man's immediate predicament and his quest for peace. In seeking relief for Middle East tensions, a return to first principles is positively advocated. In other words, the search is seriously on for a more realistic outlook, a new angle of vision. What else could prove fitting when human destiny itself is the big question mark?

Inherent in the search has been an urge to explore long-range perspectives. To that end, two specifics helped to shatter complacency. The one was that, in principle at least, social evolution in the region might come via interfaith partnership (though not syncretism). The other, that interreligious solidarity could in due course mature fuller American-Islamic co-operation.

To that end, too, the author has striven to replenish and re-tool a firsthand though modest knowledge of the field. Accessible to him for over two decades has been Princeton's fabulous intellectual armory. Favorable circumstances engendered eagerness for an assignment which otherwise might have proved impossible: the stimulus of mature minds; unexcelled documentary source material; and the leisurely yet by no means unconcerned pace of a celebrated little town.

As one brooded over the data, certain forebodings arose. For one thing, the Middle East had to be better, at any rate a little better, than perusal of the morning paper might indicate. Also, the region as a whole could be worse off, far worse off maybe, than its commonplace portrayal by optimist and enthusiast would imply. The disposition for moderation thus deepened, the desire for a fresh attack on a chronic problem took hold. The longing was heightened for such terms of reference as would guard the truth and mitigate excessive emotionalism.

Consideration of United States involvement in the region served as a starter. Of necessity, special significance attached to our relations in a part of the world called the cradle of Western civilization. A further step led right into the confines of the region. Confrontation with stark reality there can shock. It can also stab awake. For instance, it can awaken us to the genius of evil to masquerade as good. If only one knew the human tragedy as they who are its victims know!

It soon began to dawn that Middle East and world peace were one and the same. The longing for the former suggests the indivisibility of the latter. What is in the best interest of the region redounds to the self-fulfillment of all mankind. What serves the enlightened policies of the free world should shape the Middle East future.

The convulsions which rock the region reproduce, in a manner of speaking, schism in humanity's soul. They re-echo seemingly endless struggle dividing the Great Powers. But Middle East statesmanship woefully deludes itself if it succumbs to the notion that it can go it alone. No segment of the world can any longer successfully play a lone hand.

Peace and progress are apparently contingent upon inter-cultural interdependence. That in turn needs to be hammered out on the anvil of give-and-take. The organizing principle for creative reciprocity which the New Testament sets in sharp focus has not been superseded. In bare outline, it consists in love of the truth, and of neighbor as oneself.

Next in line is a direct confrontation with religion in the Middle East. This is in keeping with the assumption that religion is the core of culture. Here a sequence of four chapters helps lift the gaze to the sphere of faith where the historic Middle East has an impressive record. In what at best can be no more than a synoptic treatment, indigenous Christianity is set in bold relief. One discovers, among other things, that the three theistic religions, despite serious lapses, did achieve their own norms of coexistence long ago. The veil thus partially drawn, a close-up of regional Islam, Christianity, and Judaism is brought to view.

With that as an anchorage in comparative religion, the narrative proceeds toward its points of culmination: toward an appraisal of the modern impact of Christianity upon the region; toward an evaluation of the permanent message of medieval Arab culture, that is, what its thinkers and scientists really could mean to those who toil for a brighter tomorrow; above all, toward a rediscovery of such spiritual potentialities as might eventually minister to a better order.

In the course of reducing the above design into workable format, the author has relied, as already intimated, upon the word of authorities. In translating a set of ideas into reading matter, the temptation at times was irrepressible to transfer reflections embedded in previous writings. Particularly did this apply to a symposium he edited in 1946, *The Great Religions of the Modern World* (Princeton University Press), as well as to *The Christian Interpretation of Religion* (Macmillan, New York, 1952). Similarly, a number of positions held in certain articles of his, for example, those in *Theology Today*, fortified the strategy of the present volume.

Whether in form or substance, the finished product carries the imprint of numerous audiences who at one time or another heard its component parts. The general thesis and its corroboration emerged incalculably sharpened from two public lectures, in the summer of 1955, delivered at the Pacific School of Religion, Berkeley, California.

Textual improvements are due, furthermore, to the critical advice of several scholars who read part or all of the manuscript. Some of the early chapters came under the competent scrutiny of Dr. W. Wendell Cleland, Department of State, Washington, D.C. Expert opinion was also received from Dr. Edward Rochie Hardy, Jr., Professor of Church History, Berkeley Divinity School, New Haven, Connecticut, and Professor George F. Hourani, Department of Near Eastern Studies, University of Michigan. In much that pertains to the theory and practice of interfaith and intercultural co-operation, I am profoundly indebted to Dr. A. William Loos, Executive Director, The Church Peace Union, New York City.

A number of my advanced students at Princeton Theological Seminary rendered valuable assistance. Of these, Robert Burns Davidson, Teaching Fellow in Comparative Religion, and Rev. J. Harry Haines, of Kuala Lumpur, Malaya, made a distinct contribution.

To all these, as well as to the editors and readers of The Westminster Press, Philadelphia, Pennsylvania, my sincere gratitude and high esteem.

EDWARD J. JURJI

Princeton, N.J.

1

THE UNITED STATES AND THE MIDDLE EAST

WHAT are the essential elements in the contemporary Middle East? How does current American history, including the course taken by culture, religion, and diplomacy, impinge upon the security and destiny of the Middle East? Do these two spheres of twentieth century civilization, so different in heritage and outlook, really belong together to the extent claimed in their behalf? What is the nature of peace itself, and what are the respective roles that Americans and Middle Easterners should perform in order to make it effective? How did the great rift in American-Middle Eastern relations occur, and how can it be eliminated? How can the two regions be joined in a harmony conducive to greater stability in the whole world?

The underlying contention here is that cultural and diplomatic issues cannot be divorced from their background in the realm of religion. Being spiritual in essence, the problems that arise between America and the Middle East are universal in scope. There is more at stake than the historic Western-Oriental cleavage; indeed, we are immediately confronted with the whole future of intercultural solidarity in an atomic age.

AMERICAN IMPINGEMENT

1. Thrilled by American idealism and inwardly moved by the humanitarian virtues of individual Americans, the Arab Middle East, in the period following World War II, neverthe-

less became unusually critical of the United States' Arab policy.

Americans had been originally drawn to the region under the influence of three primary incentives. First, there was the religious and cultural motive dating from the earliest arrival of transatlantic missionaries at the Levant in 1820. By 1834, an Arabic printing press, an adjunct to the educator and evangelist, had been installed in Beirut. Exalted vision, indefatigable labor, and personnel of a high caliber, produced steady progress. The climax in this domain was reached when a number of new churches began to arise. In the educational sphere, progress was marked by the network of secondary and collegiate institutions unevenly distributed in Syria, Lebanon, Egypt, Turkey, and Iran. One of these, the Syrian Protestant College, was opened in 1866, also in Beirut. It became the justly celebrated center of higher learning which in 1919 changed its name to the American University of Beirut.

Secondly, interest in trade early in the last century began to bring Americans into contact with Middle Easterners. This is reflected in the first lines of the U.S. Marines' Hymn:

> " From the Halls of Montezuma
> To the shores of Tripoli;
> We fight our country's battles
> On the land as on the sea."

What the stanza specifically evokes is the memory of those resolute operations of 1803–1804 which our young Navy undertook in defense of American shipping against the Tripolitan corsairs of North Africa.

From that sporadic commercial relationship there developed by the turn of the century a lively trade consisting essentially in the import to the U.S.A. of unprocessed agricultural products and, later, the export from it of motor vehicles and other machinery. Dwarfing everything else was the discovery of mineral oil in Iran, Iraq, Kuwait, and Saudi Arabia, which attached global significance to the region and intensified American interest. According to Frances C. Mattison, editor of

American Interests in the Middle East, United States business investment in the countries of the Eastern Mediterranean and the Arabian Peninsula approximated up to 1950 a total of $700,000,000, of which $650,000,000 was in petroleum.

Thirdly, events originating in the period of World War II provided the basis of an even more intimate association between the United States and the Middle East. To the fundamental concern with petroleum was now added the prodigious responsibility to help maintain peace and insure the security of the free world.

American involvement began from the sound assumption that the Middle East was strategically important, the crossroads of the world connecting Asia, Africa, and Europe. President Woodrow Wilson's philosophy of self-determination had already left a profound impression in the region and, since World War I, had given encouragement to nationalist aspirations. Mainly through the efforts of Ambassador Henry Morgenthau, Cleveland Dodge, Charles R. Crane, and the American Board of Commissioners for Foreign Missions, the Near East Relief Society had been formed in 1915 to aid minority refugee groups, particularly Armenian, in the Ottoman Empire.

Issues of war and peace, of the geopolitical and geographic aspects of international relations, of air routes, world communications, and trade conspired to thrust the Middle East into the vortex of urgent business at the chancelleries. What took place in those ancient lands acquired top priority on the agenda of the great and small powers. The impingement of the United States on the Middle East ought not to be construed, however, as the revival of a discredited European colonialism. It was rather the outcome of circumstances in an atomic age which forbade the role of onlooker and spectator.

Recent history had amply demonstrated the cruciality of the region in any global struggle for power. Prior to the period of the two world wars, bitter rivalry was staged in that arena between Great Britain and Russia. It was imperative now that in the discharge of its new responsibility, the United States should substitute the strategy of a first-rate enlightened power, concerned with international organization, for that of a broker between the European powers on the one hand, and the self-conscious states and peoples of Western Asia and North Africa on the other. Great things begin to happen when the prophetic voice addresses so exalted a challenge to a nation as formidable as the United States.

2. The reasons for our failure in the Middle East may be traced to diplomatic, cultural, and religious ineptitude.

On the diplomatic front, we have alienated potential friends in the Middle East by following a foreign policy that seemed to them contradictory and confused. There are reasons, to be sure, ingrained in the soul of the Middle East, that explain its people's retreat from confidence in the United States. To that theme we will subsequently return.

In four unmistakable categories we have been shown that there is much we can learn. First, in justifiably combating Communism we tended to antagonize the masses either by declaring that nationalist movements were Moscow-inspired or by pledging support of certain reactionary and feudalist groups if only they were willing to oppose the Soviet bloc. Secondly, United States policy in recent years has favored noninterference by foreign powers and liberty for self-government. Yet we have been suspected of upholding outmoded colonialism. Thirdly, we have fallen an easy prey to the delusion that financial and technical assistance in themselves will win us the friendship of foreign states. Fourthly, in our Israel-Arab policy we have convinced the Arab world that we have tipped the scales heavily in Israel's favor.

Deeper misgivings still were evoked on the cultural side. Professor N. A. Faris of Beirut pointed out that the resultant suspicion of the United States crystallized in a feeling of fear and resentment nowhere more evident than in the case of Palestine, which became, to borrow his own idiom, " a symbol of Western, and particularly American, immaturity and bad faith in international relations."

For a period of time at least, the seriousness of our bad relationships in the Middle East eluded the intelligent American public, thanks to the slanting of the news at the hand of leading correspondents and editors. Even today our press often is relatively oblivious to the plausible aspirations of the Arab Moslem world. Whether wittingly or unwittingly, the American evangelist had, along with the gospel, distilled an applied Christianity which multitudes, shying away from conversion, had nevertheless taken seriously and believed. Then suddenly it seemed that all of idealism's solemn language was a mere façade, for even Christianity could be conveniently offered up on the altar of expediency.

The almost mortal wounds that were thus inflicted were not limited to the Middle East, but affected Asia and the entire Eastern world. Nor was that all. America's conscience became increasingly uneasy as the truth was known. Thousands of men and women who had generously given of themselves for the cause of international understanding, felt the weight of the crisis. Interest in the Middle East had literally transcended denominational and nationality boundaries in the United States.

The foremost American universities had made significant contributions to the awakening Middle East, and the degree of cultural involvement was of such a dimension that it could not be qualitatively reproduced through mere statistics. It was a living investment in the abundant life, and who can measure that? The role of Princeton University — to single out one example — suggests the universities' remarkable influence in the lands of the Eastern Mediterranean. That role is reflected in Princeton's current program in Near Eastern Studies.

Writing in 1938, Bayard Dodge, then president of the American University of Beirut, touched upon the old and fruitful intercourse between Princeton and the Middle East. "During the nineteenth century," he wrote, "most of the Near East was under the control of the Ottoman Empire. The large Christian minorities could not obtain the education which they desired and the brilliant intellectual life of Islam had become stagnant. A number of young Americans determined to spend their lives in the Ottoman territories, in order to revive the waning force of Oriental Christianity and to give to the Muhammedans a new conception of religion." (*Princeton Alumni Weekly*, November 18, 1938, p. 159.)

The seed planted in those pioneer times, when courage and devotion were magnificently displayed, yielded in due course a plentiful harvest. The men of Princeton who had joined with others in laying the foundation of a better life were followed by many. A far-reaching cultural — as well as religious — movement was set in motion. The forceful impact of American culture upon the Middle East — carefully wielded by unselfish men — passed through hard and trying days. Never was it so sorely tested, however, as in the epoch of the mid-twentieth century, and that was mainly due to the baffling contradictions in American foreign policy as well as the irrational character of Middle Eastern nationalism.

Candor demands that we concede that this religious depression in the epoch now fast drawing to a close fits rather well into the pattern of Protestant performance during the years that foreshadowed the two world wars. Four basic factors may be delineated in that connection. First, the wave of rationalism and humanism that swept through American Protestant theology. Secondly, the secularism and skepticism that seemed to gain momentum in the halls of higher learning. Thirdly, the tragic intellectual and spiritual predicament of a Church torn by the struggle between radical modernism on the one hand, and excessive fundamentalism on the other. Fourthly, a widespread fatalism with regard to the possibility that Christianity could have the least impact upon Islam.

The inevitable outcome for vital Christianity was a lowered influence in the Middle East. It all began when educators and preachers became uncertain of their distinctive message, lost conviction, and too late discovered that their position was untenable. Controversies arose, for instance, on the issue of the evolutionary hypothesis; contenders on both sides did little justice either to the cause of science or to that of faith.

A new day has at last begun to dawn. To its coming the ecumenical movement and the World Council of Churches have
greatly contributed. If the idea that there can be neither
Scythian nor Jew, neither Westerner nor Oriental, neither male
nor female, in the Church of Christ, grips the minds of all par-
ticipants in the religious drama that brings together Americans
and Middle Easterners; if a new sense of togetherness is affirmed between Moslems and Christians; if older and younger
Churches can unite in the service of the region; if the benefits
of true freedom are sought in an open society — then all the
ordeals of the moment will not have been in vain, for out of
the ashes of discord and ill-will a new page will have been
written in the history of that key region.

To peer beyond the present crisis in American-Middle East
relations is to fumble in the dark if our vision of the future ig-
nores the religious order. Apart from solid confrontation with
religion, there can be no proper reckoning with the encounter
between the Eastern world and the West. Once the smallest
break has been made in the assaulted country's tradition, one
thing inexorably goes on leading to another, as Arnold Toynbee reminds us. Precisely that is the reason why the world has
generally regarded the West with fear and trembling —
whether in pre-Soviet Russia, India, the Far East, or the
Islamic Middle East.

With most of the non-Western world, the Middle East shares
a certain degree of this fear. Nevertheless, it tends to diffract
the cultural ray emanating from the West into its component
strands — nationalism, education, technology, politics, art, and
religion. The penetrative power of a cultural strand — according to Toynbee's terminology — is in inverse ratio to its intrinsic value. Thus religion, which represents the value and
truth of a foreign cultural spectrum, is last to penetrate the
region's consciousness. A trivial strand, however, whose expression might be the cocktail party or the hair shampoo, ex-
cites little resistance and is readily assimilated.

It is a legitimate function of Christianity to moderate the

awesome power and arrogance of the West, and to dissipate the fear of the Middle East that it is a body under assault. Even as they maintain that their citizenship is in heaven, Christians ought to exercise responsibility for the West and to uphold the best in its culture, religion, and diplomacy. To the Moslem, Christianity will then convey that assurance and respect for all that is true and good in his heritage. More impressive than a thousand converts captured by the superiority of the Western tradition and the material strength of nominally Christian nations, is the faith and love inspired in one Moslem who has learned that the secret of Western culture breaks down all barriers.

Christianity needs to inspire the rulers of Western nations with a gospel that shames the futility of colonialism. It must declare the utter incompatibility with its faith of any cultural assault that disdains the proper loyalties of the Middle East. America recovers her prestige in the region as she prays for wisdom to guide, and be guided by, the peoples concerned in the way of peace. The future course of human destiny being veiled from our eyes, we all need to march together in complete surrender to the Eternal's will.

Avenues to Solidarity

There are three avenues to solidarity between America and the Middle East.

1. A diplomacy that would rightly interpret our foreign policy must proceed from the revolutionary character of American democracy. Yet American politicians repeatedly have refused to take into account the warnings sounded by every chief of mission in Egypt, Syria, Lebanon, Iraq, and Saudi Arabia of the dangers of our foreign policy apparently biased in favor of Israel. Such was the verdict of a veteran diplomat, J. Rives Childs, in an open letter to *The New York Times*, published October 27, 1953. He concluded that the seeds have been sown and that we are now reaping the whirlwind. Through the United Nations, our diplomacy gained a new world-wide

scope. Our delegates have not always been able to speak in the world organization, however, in a manner that carries conviction and wins the confidence of the Arab Moslem world.

In the years 1939–1946, our diplomats in the region were eyewitnesses to startling events. There was the establishment of the British Office of Minister of State at Cairo, and the Anglo-American Middle East Supply Center. The Axis-Vichy collaboration in Syria-Lebanon during 1941 was preceded the previous year by the German-Italian maneuver over Egypt. That was the background for the famous declaration of Anthony Eden in the House of Commons (1942) that Libya should not again come under Italian rule. A year earlier, Anglo-Soviet forces had occupied Iran.

Within that same epoch, too, Great Britain helped Lebanon free itself from France. In Morocco, the Eisenhower-Darlan story unfolded; Franklin Roosevelt revealed enthusiasm for self-determination in Morocco and for the economic open-door in Iran. The British Government increasingly yielded ground in Saudi Arabia, comforted by the fact that they were being succeeded by the United States in that oil-rich country.

With those events as a backdrop, American diplomacy ran through a progressively more turbulent course. Differences began to separate our foreign policy from those of our wartime allies, particularly on the central issue of Western penetration in the Middle East and North Africa. Toward the close of 1947, the controversy over Palestine resulted through active United States participation in the partition plan. Open support of the Jewish side in the United Nations and prompt recognition of the State of Israel in the spring of 1948 brought American diplomacy to near bankruptcy in its relations with the Arab and Moslem countries.

Objective study of the contemporary Middle East reveals that all powers involved — whether great or small — went astray. Only the U.S.S.R. and Turkey came through in the region with success in maintaining or improving their positions. Although success so far has gone to the skillful or morally ruthless, something more than the tactics of diplomacy is called for if the goal of peace and organization is to be reached. Restoration of American prestige in the region seems to be contingent upon the evolution of a foreign policy that is consistent with the revolutionary character of American democracy.

As regards the future of Israel, positive action was taken in upholding the Declaration of May 25, 1950. In that Declaration the United States had associated itself with Great Britain and France in pledging to take immediate action both within and outside the United Nations if either the Arab states or Israel was preparing to violate the frontiers or armistice lines. Beyond that the United States undertook to evolve impartial policies so as to win the respect and regard not only of Israel, but also of the Arab peoples.

These moves were truly creative and, coupled with technical assistance as well as economic aid programs, promised to win many millions to the American side. But a creative role of that order cannot become an effective instrument for peace apart from the very pertinent consideration of cultural and spiritual intercourse.

2. Solidarity between the United States and the Middle East depends in part, therefore, upon sound cultural contacts implementing the historic American tradition of freedom, equality, and the emancipation of peoples. Speaking secularly, the key word for American culture is, of course, democracy. It is that kind of democracy which the Constitution and Bill of Rights spell out, and which the Declaration of Independence proclaims. Those are the symbols and credo of our political faith as it undergirds the republic, determines our course of action, and gives purpose to our culture. Only as we generalize these assets, which form the basis of our political philosophy and bestow meaning upon the American tradition, and only as they control our multiple relations with the Middle East, will solidarity with the region result. Logic also prescribes that the Middle East itself open up to this country the assets of its cul-

ture and thus contribute its best to the solidarity we seek. That is a subject to which subsequent attention will be given.

The eminent Turkish educator Abdulhak Adnan-Adivar depicted Turkey's modern point of departure as "the official dogma of irreligion." It was not Western culture, free, critical, and democratic, that was chosen by the makers of modern Turkey. Western positivism rather, and its formula of the Good-True-and-Beautiful, was imperiously imposed on the twentieth century Turks just as Islamic dogma had been dictated to their forebears. In short, authoritarianism was as conspicuous in imposing logical positivism in the modern era as it was in the establishment of Islamic legalism when Turkey was a child. It would be, indeed, difficult to choose between Turkey's present "positivist mausoleum" and its former "dead orthodoxy." In varying degrees, the same may be said of most Middle East countries.

3. A dynamic religious strategy will have a practical appeal to the will of Middle East peoples if channeled along the lines of a campaign for peace.

This, of course, does not mean that the United States officially through its Government should evolve a religious policy toward the Middle East or any other part of the world. Professor William Warren Sweet has ably demonstrated, however, that economic and political institutions are not in themselves the main civilizing forces that shaped the destiny and formed the character of this nation.

In a presidential address before the American Historical Association (1907), Dr. J. Franklin Jameson affirmed that of all the means of estimating American character, the pursuit of religious history is the most complete.

The chief obstacle to free intercourse between this continuing American Reformation and the awakening Middle East is a historic phenomenon of endemic growth: the hardened, hereditary, and immutable antipathy between classic Christianity and classic Islam.

An Islam that conceived of Christianity as a tritheistic aberration in sharp contrast with the unadulterated theism of the Prophet's faith could scarcely come to grips with the gospel, no matter how pure the compassion and saintly the intention of the Christian witness. An Islam constantly brooding over the admittedly sub-Christian standards of Christian nations, nations now waging crusades and now producing within less than fifty years two orgies of bloodshed, is inevitably unimpressed by the magnanimity of our philanthropy. It must naturally recoil before our overtures, counting even the proclamation of the gospel as irrelevant.

A Christianity that was almost as organically brittle as Islam was necessarily unfit to minister in the Middle East. A Christianity that spurned the sincerity of Moslem seekers and ignored the massive spiritual testimony of Islamic theology was not quite ready to fathom the Islamic depth. Nor could the adherents of the two sister faiths ever conclude peace within themselves or in their common relations unless they had truly freed themselves from the patrimony of hatred. Until the artificial barriers of discord went and both Moslem and Christian in humility sought to disclose the one to the other the anxiety that lay heavily upon their consciences, their partnership was not real.

This historic antipathy is a parable of the divisive role of religion in the affairs of the world. Is there a dynamic religious strategy — applicable to both America and the Middle East — which if translated into a campaign for durable peace might lead to the gradual elimination of interfaith phobia bequeathed by centuries of distrust and open hostility?

First, without in any way presupposing the advance repudiation of their convictions, Islam and Christianity can and should join in affirming the principle of the unity of mankind. The religious concord intended to implement a peace program might thus envisage a world-wide community of free nations, upholding the principles of a free religion in a free state. There is nothing under the sun that decisively prevents men of good will everywhere from pressing for the advent of constitutional governments in the Middle East, governments that would both theoretically and positively endorse the trend toward freedom of conscience as an inalienable human right.

Secondly, relying upon high standards of education, and all the forces of true enlightenment, Christianity is certainly competent to develop in conjunction with Islam a more sensitive consciousness of republican constitutionalism in the Middle East. Turkey, Egypt, and Pakistan already have signified their formal assent to the republican type of government. Much more needs to be done from within the religious structure of Islam in order to transform what is obviously a theoretical optimum into positive, ideological dynamism. Corresponding with the American structure of society — advancing through the fruitful co-operation between the followers of a variety of creeds — American-Middle East reciprocity holds the promise of a broad cross-fertilization with happy portents for all concerned as well as for mankind as a whole.

Thirdly, whereas the above two principles underscore the philosophical and pragmatic framework for partnership between the overwhelmingly Islamic Middle East and the traditionally Christian United States, there is within Christendom itself a deeper level of action that remains relatively unexplored. The Middle East is, after all, the cradle of Christianity, and within its borders a variety of Christian sects and communions have flourished since the early centuries of Church history. In creative co-operation between American Christianity and the region's community of Christian believers, the ultimate Islamic-Christian settlement will be born.

It may not be too much to expect that through the orderly disposition of religious forces in the Middle East, the working peace we long for will at last emerge as a reality in our time. Precisely that is the fresh approach which this book suggests in presenting the religious and cultural configuration of the region.

INSIDE THE MIDDLE EAST

A N INTENSE self-consciousness has for several decades assumed revolutionary proportions in the Middle East. Whether it articulates in Turkish, Persian, Urdu, or Arabic, the region's literature reflects a flair for description with a universalism remarkable in its own right. " How can a tyrant rule the free, but for a tyranny in their own freedom and a shame in their own pride? " inquired Gibran, the Lebanese-American symbolist. Nowhere other than in international relations is this state of mind better revealed. Witness the impassioned utterances of Middle East delegates at the United Nations.

George Lenczowski specified in *The Middle East in World Affairs* the considerable impact of World War II on the process of Arab awakening which had begun a half century earlier. Syria and Lebanon gained full independence, whereas Egypt and Iraq secured Britain's consent to treaty revision. As a result of that conflict it may be said that the Middle East changed position with Eastern Europe. While Eastern European states acted as mouthpieces of the Kremlin, the Middle Eastern states did not hesitate to use the United Nations as a platform for independent action, often in opposition to the big powers.

At the root of much that moves through the Middle Eastern soul and determines the self-consciousness of the region is a historic trait: an avidity for honor among men, a craving for dignity and poise, a quality halfway between the activism of the West and the idealism of Asia. Transcended by that trait are the mores which form the motifs of religion, culture, and custom, of diplomacy, society, and ethics.

The eminent American mining engineer, K. S. Twitchell, tells in *Saudi Arabia* the story of a poor Bedouin sheik which illustrates the above-mentioned penchant of the Middle Easterner. Having lost his flocks and herds, the sheik had only one horse left. A man who had long coveted the horse and offered to buy him arrived one day and was invited to stay for a meal. When served, the guest observed an abundance of meat and a scarcity of oats and rice. Having partaken heavily of the food, he tried once more to rescue his host from penury. This time he offered to buy the horse for a much greater price than it was worth. The sheik listened attentively, then replied, " Thank you for your generosity, but we have just consumed my horse."

Analysts of this self-consciousness have often erred, however, and interpreters of the region's recent history have long strayed, when they failed to take seriously the deep religious disposition of its people. There are strong indications that the indigenous populations under study indeed believe there is a higher purpose dominant in history. Distractions of politics and superstition notwithstanding, they would readily agree that

> " There's a divinity that shapes our ends,
> Rough-hew them how we will."

Viewed from inside, the Middle East seems to call for three basic considerations. These arise in relation to the physical environment, the region's role in international affairs, and the problem of local as well as global unity.

1. No true picture of the economic and social structure of the Middle East can be projected that does not take into account the cause-and-effect relationship that exists between environment and economics, economics and society, society and politics. The Middle East constitutes the major countries of Southwestern Asia — Turkey, Iran, and Afghanistan, Iraq, Jor-

dan, Syria, Lebanon, and Israel, Saudi Arabia, Yemen, and the remainder of the Arabian Peninsula. Apart from the Nile Valley it has an area of two and a half million square miles. If Egypt, North Africa, and Pakistan were added, the region's total size would far exceed that of the United States of America.

The region has well-defined and natural barriers. To the south are the Arabian Sea and the Persian Gulf; on the west are the Mediterranean, the North African littoral, and the Sahara; northward are the Black and Caspian Seas and the equally limiting Caucasian Mountains and Turanian Desert. Geographic boundaries bar access from India.

Within this vast territory, four peripheral areas enclosing a heartland may be recognized. They are the Arabian Peninsula, Egypt-Sudan, Turkey, and Iran. The heartland, commonly known as the Fertile Crescent, comprises Palestine, Jordan, Lebanon, Syria, and Iraq, an area fought over ceaselessly and handed from conqueror to conqueror.

Rainfall, apart from a few exceptions, is entirely confined to the winter months, with scattered showers from October to May. Large areas receive less than ten inches of rain. With increasing distance from the Mediterranean inland into Asia, less and less precipitation occurs, and the aridity reaches a climax in the deserts of Arabia and Iran.

The basic economy depends on the primary products of agriculture and stock-breeding. Cultivation of high-grade cotton in Egypt has meant prosperity to a few landowners and, but for the phenomenal population increase, might have raised the average level of living. Local exports of the several countries include Israel's citrus and Dead Sea chemicals, Turkish chromium and tobacco, Iraq's dates and grain, and Iranian rugs. But the commodity that bulks largest — mainly located in the Persian Gulf zone — undoubtedly is crude oil. Petroleum deposits were estimated in 1953 as 53.3 per cent of the world's total reserves. Royalties from this source alone furnish the ruling Governments with more income than the sum of all other revenues.

This ancient human habitat is the Middle East for lack of a better name. It is probably the oldest inhabited part of Asia and the cradle of Western civilization. Although equal in area to, it has less than half the population of, the United States. Denied the blessings of industry and technology, its peoples are poor.

Semites and Indo-Europeans appeared here from the dawn of history. Today three major groupings inhabit the region. Arabic-speaking peoples are in the heartland as well as in Arabia, Egypt, Sudan, and North Africa. Turks rule Asia Minor and guard the Bosporus. Persians dwell in the famed ancient land of Iran. There are, besides, a number of minority elements distinguished in the region's annals, such as the Jews, Armenians, and Assyrians, as well as the Kurds, Afghans, and Turkomans.

The most dramatic event in the modern history of the Middle East is the migration of more than a million Jews into Palestine and the establishment of the State of Israel, while an equal number of Arabs fled their homeland. Political fragmentation, religious schisms and divisions, racial frontiers, and linguistic boundaries have sometimes had a Balkanizing effect. Yet the region as a whole does possess an underlying cultural homogeneity which obtains across most of its territories.

The Middle East was shaken out of its protracted trance by the impact of internal forces as well as by the thrust of Western liberalism and industrialism during the last century. It exhibits in the second half of the twentieth century a passion and a hunger for change. Its people seem to be unanimously agreed on one thing — pursuit of freedom in the light of their own intuitive drive for independence as well as under the enlightening stimuli of the West.

Concomitant with an unremitting struggle to wrest more from nature through progressive farming and industrial techniques is the quest of these peoples for values, meaning, and destiny. Neutralism toward Western democracy may be interpreted as the strategy of a diplomacy caught between the horns of East-West rivalry. It is the sign of the times in a region where new nations are striving for a breathing spell to gain confidence and achieve solidarity. Seen in that light, neutrality is but a maneuver. It serves as a cover for the people's revolution which favors the West and democracy yet repudiates every form of tutelage.

2. The role of the Middle East in international affairs and the drive toward peace are governed by diverse factors, of which five are sketched below.

a. *Geography and Geopolitics.* The distinctive attributes which geography has bestowed and which history has confirmed from time immemorial imply that this region must be itself. Its destiny is ever between Occident and Orient. In order to play its own role it dare not permit itself to be wholly identified with or isolated from either Asia-Africa or Europe-America. The role of a mediator is not properly understood, however, as that of a broker or middleman. He must value ideas and convictions. He must enter into the inner experience of others, share in the truth that sets men free, and join the human procession toward peace.

Solidarity with the Asian world is a matter of immense significance for the Middle East. Geographic, historic, and psychological considerations, however, conspire to forbid the complete identification of the region with the complex of Asian cultures and politics. The Western world, moreover, is inevitably drawn to Hither Asia, cradle of its faith and culture. It will not easily countenance the full Asiatization of the Bible lands. In our era, furthermore, this ancient Orient is subject to an overriding consideration inherent in its vitality to American national interests.

American involvement in Middle East affairs is due partly to the region's fabulous oil wealth and partly to its location on the map. Concern with world-wide air routes and communications is intimately related to the proximity of the land to the Soviet orbit. Geography and geopolitics do not, however, exercise finality in the determination of human destiny. If the nexus of culture, religion, and diplomacy forbids the complete immersion of the Middle East in Asia's way of life, it must of necessity stand guard also against Communist encroachment. American national security is centered today in the cradle of Western civilization. It is equally true that the self-realization of those who inhabit that cradle rests in partnership with the champions of its cultural and spiritual heritage. It is quite obvious, therefore, that the United States itself cannot limit its role to that of a mediator in a region where it can be either a friendly partner or a dreaded foe. Assuming this, we must still inquire whether American aims can be permanently attained if the United States acts in opposition to native sentiment in the region.

b. *The Course of Nationalism.* The great popular movements of Asia are, of course, spontaneous outbursts wherein the Middle East, the Indian subcontinent, and the Far East share a modicum of common ground. Yet the partition of India seems to suggest that in opposing imperialism the revolutionaries of Asia were not simultaneously committed to continental solidarity or even regional alignment.

Like any other nationalism, that of the Middle East is a fusion of local factors with external influences. It is the outcome of a historical process as well as response to new challenges. Implicit in nationalism is the liberal pattern of co-operation and freedom in an open society, as well as the irrational pattern of isolationism with all the earmarks of race, language, and culture. Recognition of this duality might help establish the affinity of the region with world-wide nationalism. It might also help evaluate, for instance, the findings of Associate Justice William O. Douglas. In *Strange Lands and Friendly Peoples* he speaks of "rumblings in every village from the Mediterranean to the Pacific."

Throughout Asia, Douglas detected a force gathering for a mighty effort. We might think, he observed in passing, that that force is Communistic, and indeed Communists are exploring the situation. But the revolutionaries are hungry men who have

been exploited from time out of mind. This is the century of
their awakening and mobilization. It is one thing to condemn
nationalism in the Middle East as irrational sound and fury,
ready to make common cause with Marxism; and it is quite another matter to discern even among the illiterate and be-
nighted masses in their surrender to mob hysteria a voice as
specific as that of our own Declaration of Independence.

Middle East nationalism rings true at several levels to the
French prototype of every modern variety. When France set
the nationalist pace for the Western world, it combined eighteenth century humanitarian cosmopolitanism with the novel
idea of a sovereign nation-state. This dynamic ferment which
swept Europe was capable within twenty years of transforming Germany and Italy. The impact of German literature upon
Russia — taking the philosophical writings of Johann Gottfried
von Herder as a case in point — became the heady wine that
intoxicated and rejuvenated the intellectual life of the Slavs.
Herder drew the picture of the docile and irenic Slavs as victims of warrior nations such as Germany.

A chain reaction thus set in motion spread from Europe to
Asia. The liberal outlook of Hindus such as Gandhi and Tilak
placed the latter at the outset of his career in the contradictory
position of repudiating European civilization though not British rule. Chinese resistance to the West broadened into a
wholesale refusal to permit any intercourse between China
and the outside world. Japan, much like Prussia (after 1806)
and Russia (after 1928), adopted with remarkable dexterity
and success the forms of industrial life and efficient administration. Planned and controlled by the states, these reforms were
only in exceptional cases the outcome of individual initiative.
The ultimate objective invariably was to protect the national
heritage. The degree of Westernization was gauged to the
power produced in defense of the native cultural traditions
against the West.

The story of nationalism in Great Britain and the United
States needs to be recalled at this point. Here, not unlike

France, the beginnings are in the evolution of self-government. Here also the social and political rejuvenation preceded, or at least accompanied, the cultural awakening of the nation. It may be said that the epic of Anglo-American nationalism was largely one of internal or immanent growth — product of native social and political forces. In the case of Great Britain, nationalism made gradual adjustments to the needs and demands of a polyglot empire. In the United States it proceeded against many strains and stresses in a new environment which absorbed the various immigrant nationalities in an atmosphere of relative security and an economy of increasing plenty.

How did nationalism thrive in the Middle East? At first glance, modern Turkey's adventure might suggest itself as model for the Iranian, Pakistan, and Arab experiments. Turkey was the extreme opposite of China, in that under Mustafa Kemal it eagerly sought and encouraged intercourse with the West. To most observers the Turkish Republic stands as a monument to full acquiescence in parliamentary methods, individual rights and responsibilities, representative government, woman's suffrage, public education, separation of religion and state, and establishment of free institutions.

Turkey not only stood for complete Westernization; it actually proclaimed itself part of the West, a Western nation within a Middle East setting. The erstwhile interminable duel between Westernism and Orientalism was thus concluded. After a transitional dictatorship, Turkey entered upon a firm alliance with the democratic West. The state whose head was in the nineteenth century known as the Sick Man of Europe, by 1954 became the Well Man of NATO.

When Kemal determined to adopt the Latin alphabet, he called in Turkey's foremost scholars and asked them how long it would take the citizenry to switch over from the Arabic script. Following lengthy discussion, the learned men estimated that it would take six years. *Life* rephrased the retort of modern Turkey's founder: " Well," he said, " just assume that five years and a half have elapsed." It is this fairly optimistic view of Turkey's upheaval that has quite frequently closed the eyes of investigators to the less attractive aspects of its culture and religion. Between 1947 and 1953 the United States invested more than a billion dollars in Turkey, and the Turks have made splendid use of this help. The Turkish Army emerged as one of the best in Europe. In 1950 there were free elections; the opposition beat the party that had been in office for twenty-seven straight years.

Although an integral part of the region, modern Turkey is by no means the key to the understanding of nationalism in the Middle East. This assertion should not preclude the possibility that in the next several decades Turkey's example might prove to be normative for other Islamic states. As of the present moment, however, Turkey does not sufficiently reflect — on the deepest level — issues distinctive of the area as a whole. As regards Iran, Afghanistan, and Pakistan, moreover, they represent the transition stage toward veritable Asian life, and are in fact peripheral to the Middle East rightly so-called. If so, that must leave the several Arab states as the field confronted with this particular nationalism.

Except for the qualitatively French ideas of humanitarian cosmopolitanism and the concept of the nation-state, Arab nationalism stems from protracted brooding over the glorious records of Islamic history. In contrast to its Turkish counterpart, the Arab revolution, save for sporadic outbursts of violence and petty wars, has been comparatively bloodless and peaceful. Hence the comparison of Egyptian Abdel Nasser with Ataturk is not strictly accurate.

Nor has Arab nationalism been bolstered by considerable industrialization. The advent of civil liberties, freedom of conscience, and the parliamentary process has been rather fitful and slow. Religious institutionalism is still the formal criterion for the structuring of society. The essence of this nationalism draws heavily upon the classical forms, and is discovered in commitment to the ideals of a renaissance conceived as the continuation of the medieval caliphates of Medina, Damascus, Baghdad, Cordova, and Cairo.

The Arab states suffer from the drawback that, despite the Arab League, their common life and aspirations lack a united front. In potentialities for the future ordering of Middle East society, the League offers immense possibilities, although its record to date has been largely academic and fraught with too many rifts to be effective. As long as this type of fragmentation persists, any large-scale mobilization of the area's natural resources for the benefit of all, and any endorsement of unity with Asia or the West, must remain a diplomatic gesture.

c. *Islamic Law.* The reader will have seen already that the Middle East shares with Asia two kinds of orientation related to our subject. First, a nationalism that finds its crux in a culturalism intent upon the revivification of its parent traditions and then ingrafting from the West the techniques necessary to raise the living standards of the masses. Secondly, the rejection of Western control in any form whatever. But the recovery of its heritage means that Islamic law, the core of Middle East religion and culture, must be reinterpreted and adjusted to modern conditions. And such a resuscitation must increasingly call for a new basis of communion with Asia's cultures.

Professor F. S. C. Northrop briefly sketched in *The Meeting of East and West* and set forth more incisively in *The Taming of the Nations* the close kinship of Islam with the theoretic, determinate, theistic, and articulate faiths of the West. Islam the faith may be defined as a religion that incorporates beliefs common to the earlier Semitic religions, Judaism and Christianity. It specifies and proclaims such beliefs in the light of what it accepts as the special revelation that God gave in the Koran through the instrumentality of Mohammed. Islam the state must then be one that upholds the Koran and Tradition as the central organizing principle in national and international affairs. Islam the culture must likewise draw its true spirit from the same revealed truth. Islamic law is that system of legislation grounded in the revealed truth of the Koran. It developed with the aid of reason, inference, analogy, and consensus of opinion, and was interpreted in accordance with the demands of a changing world.

Islam the faith inculcates, and its law assumes, two basic principles. First, that nature and man are the creation of God — omniscient, personal, eternal, and transcendent in character. Secondly, that each individual person has a soul immortal and determinate, that is, different from any other.

This monotheistic conception of God and man is entrenched in a third principle which pertains to justice formulated into universal laws. Indeed, like the West, but conspicuously unlike most of Asia, Islam conceived of justice as the governing of individual persons. It also envisaged the settlement of disputes under codes, commandments, and rules — rooted in the Koran and Tradition and constituting the official standards of the community. Construed as universal and of divine origin, these laws make all men equal before God.

d. *Asia's Way of Life.* Five principal patterns of existence vie with each other in contemporary Asia. The Islamic pattern has just been touched upon. The Communist pattern is paramount particularly in Asiatic Russia and Red China. The social philosophy which Mr. Nehru projects through his secular state constitutes a third way of life hitherto unknown in Asia. Side by side with these is Western democracy with all its implications and associations; it is represented not only by the remaining colonial regimes, but by various local groups and individuals scattered across the continent. Fifthly, there is that truly Asian way of life dramatically popularized by such reformers as Gandhi.

The last category is by far the most widespread and inclusive pattern of life which makes sense to the ordinary Asian. It harks back to a non-Aryan Indian origin, and is enshrined in the Bhagavad-Gita (the song celestial), regarded as the New Testament of Hinduism. This way of life has an expression in ahimsa (nonviolence) and is the unifying world outlook of India and the Far East. In it the common denominator of Hinduism, Buddhism, Confucianism, and Taoism is embodied.

Distinctive of this veritably Asian way of life is the longing, not to transform human nature, but rather to find oneself in the world as it is. Joined to that quest is the basic conviction that all things in the world of objects are transitory. The one thing in man and nature that abides, and to which absolute commitment is due, is conceived as an impersonal, unknowable, ultimate reality. This reality is recognized by the Hindu as Brahman, and by the Buddhist and Taoist in terms of Nirvana and the Tao, respectively. Hence the pragmatic philosophy of Asia. It spells out the meaning of life through an immediate world which must be enjoyed while it lasts, and through an ultimate one which can only be surmised but never apprehended.

This discrepancy between India and the Far East, on the one hand, and the Middle East and the West, on the other, is nowhere more clear-cut than in the realm of law and morality. Having regard for the impermanence of man and his world, Asia declares the relativity of all laws and regulations that apply to persons, conditions, societies, and nations; its philosophy of law and morality goes beyond the rules and prescriptions to consider the ways and means of introducing mediation and accommodation. Its main objective is justice through the settlement of disputes and morality through mutual good will.

The Middle East and the West stand in marked though not absolute discontinuity with all that. Whether in the Old Testament, Islamic law, or the Roman and Christian West, there is a concept of justice keyed to revealed truth and eternal purpose. In the settlement of disputes between men and nations, persons and parties are measured and made equal before a common law. In so far as morality is concerned, an absolute line of demarcation is drawn between the righteous and the evil, the virtuous and the villain. Seekers of unity in the Middle East and unifiers of the world need to probe more accurately the nature of this discontinuity between Asia and the West.

e. *The Vision and Power of the West.* The vision of the West has accompanied its traditional culture from Plato and Aristotle down to the present. Enriched and reinforced by Christianity, it was given a new transforming power. Its basic affirmation is that a spiritual realm beyond the phenomenal is creative, personally and corporately, giving purpose and meaning to history and human destiny. Neither spatial nor temporal, this spiritual, immaterial realm imposes upon culture and religion some of its characteristics, bestowing vision and power.

The British philosopher C. E. M. Joad described in *Decadence* the nonhuman, immaterial, spiritual elements in the universe as the true object of man's vision. He also suggested that decadence in the Western world might be depicted as the failure of man to read accurately his position in the universe. This misreading consists in failure to acknowledge the nonhuman elements of value and deity as the proper object of deep dedication. In other words, a culture is decadent when it drops the object of all being and thus loses both vision and power. Reinhold Niebuhr characterizes the cultures of Asia as " sleeping-waking cultures in which the drama of human history is not taken seriously, and in which nature is either deified or reduced to a value of illusion." But he feels constrained to compare Communism — introducing itself to Asia as a harbinger of great hope — with the apparent contradictions in the various Western cultural, religious, and political imports.

Culture within a given ethnic area is the practice and expression of what is maintained as the intellectual and spiritual core of that civilization. For the West, the reality of culture must culminate in a vision, affirmed and shared on the personal, national, and international levels. Power is received when decadence is checked through attachment to the nonhuman elements of value and deity in history. Seen in that light, the contradictions of Western culture are tempered if not canceled out.

This is true of the central contradictions that beset us. It applies to the contradiction between the Christian faith expounded by the missionary enterprise and the cult of science professed in the academic centers of the West; to the contradiction between the idealism expressed by ecclesiastical statesmanship and the imperial impulse of lustful states; and to the contradiction between our cherished piety and evil principalities in high places.

Having ascertained the real source of its vision and rediscovered the nature of power, the West must still forestall retreat and prevent decadence through action on world-wide frontiers. It is no longer true that Asia and the Middle East are represented by backward races whom to serve best is to leave undisturbed. Today the Orient is astir with a new dynamism that challenges our finest thought and deepest concern. Either we resolve the riddle of our relations with Asia, or we are indirectly threatened with decadence by default. As a preliminary step in that direction, let us recall that politics deals with the proximate ends of life, religion with the ultimate. The same solemn wisdom that forbids either politics or religion from being vested with the sanctity of the other, prescribes that the two should complement and not neutralize each other.

Americans who have mastered this lesson in their own national life need feel no great qualms in translating it in terms of the interdependence of all cultures. It is precisely at this point that we begin to know the full meaning of our relation to Asia and the Middle East.

It will require both vision and cultural versatility to establish a fruitful relationship with India, for example. Prime Minister Nehru was able to carry most of non-Islamic Asia with him because he satisfied the Asian ideals of the superior man as a mediator. It was in compliance with that requirement that Nehru refused to take sides in the Korean War or in the wider contest between liberal democracy and Communist totalitarianism. Galling as neutrality in this case must be to us, we must nevertheless rise to the occasion and welcome the Indian role of mediator, if only because it stems from the doctrine that prescribes the settlement of disputes, an Asian principle which in the moments of our crisis we dare not disparage.

The Islamic Middle East, too, presents unique opportunities for partnership in coexistence and the practice of international as well as intercultural fellowship. Islam has been regarded – due to its determinate universal law – as the most vital religious factor in Asia. Inspired by such a law, Moslems were shocked to their heels to see what they considered a miscarriage of justice in Palestine. Embittered by their defeat and humiliated by centuries of foreign domination, the followers of the Prophet are seeking to restate their case and so reaffirm their brotherhood. In the next half century Pakistan, Malaya, and Indonesia will seek to clarify their Islamic heritage drawn from the Middle East. Together with other coreligionists – inhabiting strategic lands extending from Morocco to the Philippines – Moslems might well determine the outcome of war and the nature of peace.

To work with, not against, the Islamic concept of the Divine as compassionate in feeling and forthright in deed, does not involve the abandonment of those elements of strength in Western culture and religion. On the contrary, it means the extension to the Middle East of the principles of a free society: freedom and equality for all; religious liberty; and the separation of Church and State.

It is essentially this exalted vision of man and his destiny that is actually creative throughout Asia today. Western Christian culture – rejected as alien and scoffed at in many Asian quarters – is far from completely forgotten in the Middle East and the Far East. It is represented in almost every village by some indigenous person who may be counted upon to understand the West because the vision and power of its nondecadent culture have been disclosed to him.

3. The unity of the East, like that of the West, ultimately is one of interdependence not merely in economics but also in cultural outlook. Yet intercourse between individuals and societies, as Alfred North Whitehead discerningly pointed out, takes one of two forms, force or persuasion. The worth of men consists in their liability to persuasion. Commerce is the great example of intercourse by persuasion.

A radical reorganization of production effort and considerable capital investment are needed in the Middle East where population presses upon scanty resources. Otherwise the elementary necessities of life cannot be produced in sufficient quantity. Water and electric power are desperately needed. To provide the first, dams must be built, and the second is an indispensable supplement to human muscles. Decisive, too, in the immediate future will be the impact of Western economics, directly by its foreign operations, and indirectly by the demand on raw materials.

The distinguished Beirut economist, Professor Said B. Himadeh — referring to the economic situation in the Arab Middle East — noted that trade among the countries of the area was at a minimum. Partly due to the production of identical goods, this lag in interstate commerce originates in the pursuit of economic self-sufficiency within each independent country. Despite the avowed purpose of the Arab League to set economic co-operation as a goal, as it is solemnly stated in its pact, it has not succeeded as yet in the abolition of trade barriers. Lack of vitality in interregional trade continues to discourage large-scale production and the advantage of reduced costs is sacrificed.

Emile Bustani, Lebanon's parliamentarian, proposed in 1953 that income from Arab oil should yield profit and offer lasting prosperity to the whole region if judiciously invested within the area. To that end, he advanced the view that the establishment of an Arab Development Bank wherein revenue from oil would be deposited might go a long way in resolving the economic stringency of the Arab world. Self-liquidating schemes might then be undertaken, for example, hydroelectric projects to serve the nascent manufacturing industry, and arteries of transportation which would foster wider trade and communication and open up extensive marketing opportunities. The construction and upkeep of dams, canals, highways, railroads, telephone and telegraph circuits might conceivably relieve the staggering unemployment and mitigate the tragic lot of the refugees.

That the hope for peace was inexorably linked to economic integration was the philosophy of Andrew Carnegie, who in 1900 built the Peace Palace at The Hague. The collapse of nineteenth century peace dreams served a belated notice on all governments that there could be no peace if failure on the economic front persisted.

In so far as the Middle East is concerned, some internationalists conceived of an Israel which would emerge as an industrial center of destiny, an instrument of regional rehabilitation. This dream has been entirely unrealized; and there exists instead the Arab refugee problem: a million former citizens of Palestine, deprived of their human rights, living within view of their ancestral homes but unable to return to them. That was a historic example of the total breakdown of interdependence. Further east, around the shores of the Persian Gulf, however, lay the world's richest oil fields, where not the Industrial Revolution alone, but new scientific, educational, and economic revolutions were in full swing. In a strange land, governed still by the strict observance of the Koran, the unity of interdependence became a living reality.

The conclusion seems inescapable. When the vigorous efficiency of the engineer and the subtle calculations of the economist are matched by imaginative youth represented in awakened Governments willing to participate in regional agricultural and industrial developments; and when the Western powers concerned shall have boldly determined to uphold the doctrine of the interdependence of peoples, the unity of the Middle East, and good will in the entire world, shall have a new birth.

Hence our stand inside the Middle East has led to a confrontation with the deep issues of its religion and culture. Among other things, it has involved us in the need to ponder within those ancient ramparts the juxtaposition of Islam, Christianity, and Judaism.

ISLAM: A RELIGIOUS TRADITION

A NY attempt to comprehend the Middle East apart from knowledge of its Islamic religious tradition is bound to fail. Currently the region is represented by peoples who in their daily lives reflect a nontechnical culture in a world whose overriding cultural principle is technical. As a refuge for the bewildered Middle Eastern soul, the Islamic religious tradition thus acquires extraordinary significance.

This Islamic religious tradition is a mighty historical force. It is one of the very rare traditions that bridged the gap between Asia and Europe. Were Westerners able to grasp the Islamic genius of the Middle East, and were Middle Easterners to comprehend the inherently Christian core of Western culture, the question of coexistence on this planet might be more easily resolved.

An introduction to Islam as a religious tradition might be attempted under its three components: faith, law, and works.

FAITH

The Islamic religious tradition is a faith centered in scripture, worship, theology, and ethics.

1. For scripture, Islam has the Koran, of which the Cairo theologian Mohammed Abduh (1849–1905) wrote: "In the early epoch of Islam, scholars recognized the power of the Koran in captivating the hearts of men, and they came to the conclusion that the faith will not endure without the Koran. To

this verdict further confirmation was added when the inter-
mingling of the Arab with the other races was under way. Like
their Arab coreligionists, foreign converts to Islam came to
appreciate the imperative need to retain the integrity of the
Arabic language. Accordingly, they applied themselves to the
study of its literature and reduced its grammar to writing. . . .
I, for one, would assert that the Koran is God's miraculous
proof of his truthful religion. Islam cannot live without a sound
understanding of the Koran, based upon the continuity of Arabic." (*Great Religions of the Modern World,* by Edward J.
Jurji, p. 184, Princeton University Press.)

This elevated conception of scripture is in keeping with the
Koran's own claims:

" That is the Book: there is no doubt therein; a guide to the
pious who believe in the unseen [2:1, 2]. . . . And if ye are in
doubt of what We have revealed to our servant, then bring a
chapter like it [2:21]. . . . These are the signs of the perspicu-
ous Book. Verily, We have revealed it, an Arabic Koran; haply
ye may understand. We shall recount to thee the best of sto-
ries, as We reveal to thee this Koran [12:1–3]. . . . Thou
couldst not recite before this any Book, nor write it with thy
right hand [29:47]. . . . Had We sent down this Koran upon
some mountain, thou wouldst have seen it, humbling itself and
cleaving assunder for fear of God: These parables We speak to
the people, haply they may think [59:21]." (*The Koran,* tr. by
E. H. Palmer, Oxford University Press, London.)

Intrinsically, the doctrine that the Koran is the uncreated
word of God strikes one as a singular parody on the Johannine
disclosure: " In the beginning was the Word, and the Word
was with God, and the Word was God." The implication is one
of ultimate borrowing of the logos idea from Greek thought or,
more plausibly, the concept of God's Word from the Hebraic
prophetic tradition.

This Book is one of boundless spiritual power in the lives of
Moslems. Basically, the " Mohammedans " are worshipers of
God, but in a real sense also they are " Koranists." No one, save

by its authority, may speak about the spiritual realm. Ever since the appearance of the Koran, Islam has come into being, a religion without an ecclesia, without a central see. There is no sacramental clergy, no priestly caste. Anyone, without the laying of hands or any other form of bequeathing or sharing the sacerdotal office, may become a mosque imam or member of the conclave of divines.

2. Islamic worship provides further self-disclosure of the faith's spiritual potential.

Whether in the profession of faith, wherein the sole God and the last Prophet are confessed; the rendering of alms, an embodiment of charity into law; the fast, an abstinence from food and base thoughts by day; or the annual pilgrimage, a gathering of multitudes of the faithful from their far-flung habitats, crying, " *Labbayka* " (" Here I come! ") at the birthplace of the faith, the worshipful spirit permeates everything. Prayer is Islam's noblest contribution to moral vigor and spiritual elevation.

The standing posture, alternating with kneeling and prostration, accompanied by Koranic recitation, adoration, and praise, is pervaded by a profound humility and devotion, making for spiritual expansion. Though the face is turned toward Mecca and a fixed order of worship is followed in most communities, the form of prayer was not to become a matter of dispute: " To God belongs the East and the West; whichever way ye turn, the face of God is there. Verily God is unrestricted, knowing " (*ibid.*, 2:109).

When intoxicated persons, causing disorder, were discovered at the worship services, the use of wine was restricted, later prohibited. Along with almsgiving, prayer came to be a manifestation of Islamic piety. The Islamization of the Arab was made possible largely by means of ritual prayer. Through it today millions of Moslems in many lands open their inner selves to the working of a higher life.

Whether in solitude or in the congregation of the faithful, five times daily, at dawn, noon, midafternoon, sunset, and evening, they seek to express their yearnings in the awful presence of Allah. The greater consciousness of solidarity which communal prayer engenders is enlarged as the armies of pilgrims from distant lands worship together around the central mosques of Mecca. Even upon an outsider, the contagious solemnity, decorum and humility regnant at a Moslem divine service leave a profound impression.

Prayer, according to a Moslem Tradition, is like a stream of fresh water, flowing beside the gate of each believer. Into it the worshiper plunges five times a day and no impurity can cling to him after so much washing. But the most gracious thing ever said about Moslem prayer is that it is an intimate converse with God. A creative force in Islam, it has fostered a feeling of equality among the believers. It mitigates the rankling sense of race superiority and caste and opens a new inlet for the entry of mystical experience into the Moslem heart.

3. Theology is also a focus of the Islamic tradition of faith. The entire gamut of Islamic theology is determined by the doctrine of Allah, which places the greatest stress on his uniqueness and unity: " Say: He is God, one; God, the eternal; he begetteth not nor was begotten. Coequal with him there hath never been anyone " (*ibid.*, 112: 1–4).

Nor was it an abstract, philosophical concept of God that Mohammed proclaimed when he enunciated the great affirmation: " There is no deity but Allah." Rather was it the positive, personal declaration of faith in the Lord over all. Nothing exists apart from him and his handiwork. The Koranic conception of God includes, among other elements, a clear-cut assertion of his creativeness, knowledge, omnipotence, and eternity.

A clue to God's dealings with men is offered in the formula prefacing every Koranic chapter: " God the merciful, the compassionate." His pervasive ultimacy is cosmic like light. " God is the light of the heavens and the earth; his light is like a niche in which is a lamp, the lamp in glass and the glass like a glittering star lit from a blessed tree, an olive neither of the East nor of the West, whose oil would almost give light even though no fire did touch it; light upon light; God guideth to his light whom he willeth; God coineth parables for the people, and God everything doth know " (*ibid.*, 24:35). Man's relation to him is one of complete dependence.

The gap between God's transcendence and his immanence remained a problem of theologians for many centuries. The gradual merging of the world with Allah is largely the product of Sufi mysticism. Meanwhile, the problem of God's personality exercised the scholastic minds. Step by step they divested Allah of his creation until it was difficult to discern his relevance to the world.

Another important phase of this theology relates to the problem of providence. There was evolved a doctrine of predestination which ordinarily came to suggest man's accidental, perhaps even haphazard, exposures to divine caprice and might. A determinism of this kind reached an all-time low when divine sovereignty and human freedom were set in mutual opposition.

In a spiritless and skeptical age, the further deterioration of the once vibrant doctrine of God's sovereignty could sink to the level of kismet (lot, portion), especially that of the well-known Turkish brand. This in reality was not an expression of theological doctrine, but a fatalistic mood which accepted with resignation " the slings and arrows of outrageous fortune." In fairness one must admit that in Mohammed's conception of God's sovereign power there is encountered, not a weak doctrine, but a profound and majestic view of Almighty God and his relation to the world of men. It is with no small measure of certainty regarding the essence of their faith that competent theologians of Islam admonish their folk to shake off an unworthy interpretation of providence.

4. Islamic ethics, in its broad, world-wide manifestation, seems to follow a set of patterns fixed by the Prophet and amplified later. Involved is tension between a purely religious motive and one based on the merit and reward principle. Further tension arises between, on the one hand, the hedonism be-

queathed by Arab materialism, a certain interpretation of the
Prophet's sex life, and the Koranic picture of a sensuous bliss
in paradise, and, on the other, the Prophet's austere piety and
the ascetic, devotional example of his daily life. This ethical
dualism notwithstanding, man's dutiful response to God's gifts
is governed by a profound sense of gratitude. Resignation to
one's lot is deemed an imperishable treasure.

Other elements in the Islamic ethic reflect an old Arab origin
magnified in the cherished virtues — bounty, chivalry, forbear-
ance, hospitality, magnanimity, and patience. The position of
Mecca as a powerful commercial metropolis, with established
doles for the poor and sick, might have contributed in part to
the early Islamic interest in philanthropy. Study of the traits
of man's moral character was developed into a didactic science
permeated by Greek peripatetic insight. The underlying assumption was that certain vices must be weeded out and
changed by proper nurture.

Among the virtues to which students of ethics give space
were delight of the soul, exalted thought, liberality, tender-
ness, chastity, friendship, and sociability. The moral weak-
nesses which were commonly recognized included envy, jealousy, anger, intemperance, arrogance, and falsehood.

Moslems have always stood as uncompromising prohibition-
ists, and the Wahabi firebrands of Arabia in their inflexible
zeal have outlawed tobacco also. A watchful eye is kept on
sexual laxity. Polygamy, rare in the urban centers today, is understood as an attempt to curb rather than relax man's inborn
lust. It is also regarded by Moslem thinkers as an attempt to
grant respectability to the surplus women in the community.
The veiling of women and their seclusion, going against the
grain of Arabian custom, represent in reality the restoration of
an ancient Semitic practice. Reflected in the Code of Ham-
murabi, this institution expressed the desire of Mohammed
and the early believers to catch up with the higher Byzantine
and Persian cultures.

Islamic morality is guided all along the line by the desire to work for the cleansing of one's soul in order that man may thereby be pleasing to God. The ultimate goal of the conscientious Moslem is so to live that the weight of sin may be offset on the Day of Reckoning by his good works.

LAW

Islamic justice is the privilege of the believer. It purports to affirm the rights of the poor and humble, but shirks any serious responsibility for those outside the pale. In Greek civilization two opposing conceptions of justice arose. There was, first, the popular notion expounded in the tragedies. A second was advanced by the philosophers, Plato and Aristotle in particular; it freed the idea of justice from popular religion, retaining its connection with morality. Almost the reverse happened in Islam. Here a tentative separation was effected between justice and morality, but justice and religion were regarded as one and inseparable.

Pursuing the comparisons between Islam and the classical tradition a step farther, we might recall that Greece finally evolved Stoic justice. This was a transition toward the Roman emphasis on individual justice. Regarding the law as impersonal in origin, the Greeks had conceived of it as a conclusion of reason and not an expression of will.

Roman jurisprudence ascribed the character of law to either a conclusion of reason or an expression of will. This progressive enhancing of the volitional element finds its explanation in the importance, respectively, of the Roman Emperor and the Christian God as concepts dominating human reflection.

It is doubtful whether Islamic justice could ever have become what it is had it depended entirely upon the contents of the Koran and Tradition. Even the advent of analogical deduction, consensus of opinion, the legal right of interpretation, and private legal opinion would not have availed, or have been possible, but for the process of borrowing from outside sources.

As late as the autumn of 1953, however, members of the Colloquium on Islamic Culture, held at Princeton, found themselves divided on the central issue of Islamic law. The Turkish jurists could dispense with the sacred law as the regulatory basis of the communal life of the nation. But the majority of other Moslem delegates affirmed that Islam, being a way of life, lays down the basic principles that are indeed applicable in a changing world.

The transition from Stoic philosophy to that of the Roman jurists may be compared superficially with the transition experienced by the Arabs when their desert morality gave way to a system of justice under Islam.

In Islam, the cumulative character of justice is evident. In its fundamental nature, however, Islamic justice is more reminiscent of Hebrew thought, since like the latter it passed through three stages:

1. Social justice, imposed and sanctioned by God;
2. Religious justice;
3. Eschatological justice.

At its root, moreover, there is an all-pervading mystical spirit. This profound mystical disposition is regarded by certain observers as an irrational impediment to the proper grasp of Islamic law. It is precisely that phase of the subject however, which affords us an approach to the vast maze before us.

Within the content of its law, Islam reveals itself as an heir to Middle Eastern antiquity and medievalism, a monotheistic faith, and world-religion and culture today. In the Middle East took place the mingling of the Indo-European from the north with the Mediterranean from the south, which produced the art, culture, and law of the Greeks and Romans. And there, on the Semitic verge of Asia, home of religious enthusiasms from the beginning, arose Christianity.

Islam and its land appear as the Eastern branch of Western civilization, forming a sector of that fairly homogeneous sphere of cultures and religions embracing Western Asia and Europe. Together with the West, Islam enjoys the legacies of Greek culture and Hebrew religion.

Yet the Islamic legal system has an independent and proper

value of its own. It is linked to the same religious tradition
that is back of our own American system of government. It is
based on the assumption that there are certain absolute values,
referred to in the Declaration of Independence as the " Laws
of Nature and of Nature's God."

When Chief Justice Vinson of the Supreme Court said in a
1951 opinion, " Nothing is more certain in modern society than
the principle that there are no absolutes," Christians took note.
This false doctrine espoused by the Chief Justice got its start
with the late Justice Oliver Wendell Holmes. It is an idea that
has come down from the Harvard Law School, which Holmes
dominated, and has penetrated deep into the Government at
Washington. In this respect, Islamic law rests on a firmer foundation.

Admittedly, Mohammed did not establish a legal system to
regulate the life of his followers. During his lifetime the old
Arabian customary law continued to exist. It was based mainly
upon Semitic tribal law, modified in the course of adaptation
to different social conditions and containing foreign elements
of provincial Roman and perhaps Mesopotamian and South
Arabian provenience.

With the Prophet's death, the issuance of Koranic and extra-
Koranic legislation ceased. The first few caliphs tried to direct
the community in the spirit of the founder. But as a result of
the vast territorial acquisitions, it was inevitable that the law
that the Arabians had imported with themselves should prove
insufficient.

A Moslem is nevertheless bound by religious regulations.
This is so not only in the performance of the daily ritual prayers, in the fast, the pilgrimage to Mecca, and other religious
rites. It also is the case in contraction and dissolution of marriage, in commercial contracts, as well as in domestic and social life. All these regulations came in the course of time to be
welded together in a code of law. This is called Sharia (the
way), that is, that way which the faithful must follow.

Meanwhile there emerged four orthodox juridical schools of

Islamic law which together constituted a system of religio-juridical thought. All the obligations the Koranic law had imposed upon the Moslem in his triple capacity of believer, man, and citizen of a theocracy came to be formulated under the label of *fiqh* (wisdom), the *juris prudentia* of the Romans.

The earliest and largest school is the Hanafite, so named after abu-Hanifah (d. 767). He flourished in al-Kufah and Baghdad, and his system is the most tolerant. A conservative school, the Malikite, was founded by Malik ibn-Anas (c. 715–795) in Medina. In between the just-named liberal and conservative schools is the Shafiite school founded by Mohammed al-Shafii (d. 820, in Cairo).

A fourth legal system is the Hanbalite, taking its name from Ahmad ibn-Hanbal (d. 855, in Baghdad). The extreme conservatism of this group served to make it the bulwark of orthodoxy in Baghdad against rationalist innovations. It was revived by ibn-Taymiyah (1263–1328), and in the eighteenth century became standard for the Wahabis and eventually the law of Saudi Arabia.

According to their traditional unsystematic arrangement, the textbooks of these schools devote the first chapters to the five principal religio-ritual obligations. This is usually followed by contracts, inheritance law, criminal law, the holy war and relations with unbelievers in general, dietary laws, sacrificial and slaughter rules, oaths and vows, court procedure, and the freeing of slaves.

Not all these regulations involve obligatory prohibitions or commandments. In many cases it is merely desirable or reprehensible from the religious standpoint to omit or to do something. The law also regulates actions which it leaves open as permissible or neutral. Such a religious valuation has largely superseded the juridical categories proper.

Almost half of Islam in the world today professes the Hanafite jurisprudence. The Shafiite school comes next in number of adherents. The Malikite school, once predominant in Moslem Spain, at present prevails in northern and western Africa with the exception of Lower Egypt, and in the Sudan as well as in the Arab zone bordering the Persian Gulf.

In the Ottoman Empire only the Hanafite rite was official; and today the lands that were once Ottoman, as well as those of central Asia and Pakistan, follow Hanafite law. In matters of personal status, therefore, the Islamic community of the Middle East, with several important exceptions, follows the Hanafite rite. The exceptions include Turkey, which has set aside Islamic law, the Shiites (sectarians), who observe a sacred Moslem legislation of their own, and Saudi Arabia, which upholds the Hanbalite system. Non-Moslems are generally free to institute their own religious courts.

Every Sunnite (orthodox) Moslem ordinarily belongs to one of the four schools of jurisprudence and conducts himself in accordance with its precepts. But he is not tied to it for life; he is permitted to pass from one school to another. In the same family, father and son may belong to different schools. Yet this broad and meticulous system of law never quite succeeded in translating its claims of absolute validity into practice. Even in countries where Moslems enjoyed self-government, the state could not refrain from laying down a complete code of independent secular law, designed to meet the changing times.

Secular powers increasingly assumed jurisprudence in matters of constitutional, military, financial, economic, and educational policy. The whole sphere of international relations, being subject to partnership in the world community, represented a new departure in Islamic political theory. Thus throughout the Middle East there has arisen a twofold administration of justice, the one religious, the other secular. And that is how Islamic jurisprudence tended to become rather academic, mainly concerned with an ideal.

WORKS

Under the heading of works are envisaged the motivation and performance of those who subscribe to the Islamic religious tradition. Not infrequently today, Islamic performance stands out for contradiction and recalcitrance; and these are grounded, in so far as motivation goes, in the deeper considerations of ultimate reality and the conception of man.

1. *The Contradictory Character of Islamic Thought and Culture.* Contradiction between the secular and the spiritual orders of modern Islam is quite obvious. The great Egyptian thinker Taha Hussein, in *The Future of Culture in Egypt,* laid bare the nature of contradiction between Islam-the-faith and Islam-the-culture. He stated along the following lines the contradiction between Cairo's al-Azhar, Islam's leading theological university, on the one hand, and Egyptian higher education, on the other.

As the foremost center of Islamic learning, he argued, al-Azhar ought to be the throbbing heart of culture in the Arab-Moslem world. Actually, it is far from being articulate as such. Al-Azhar should inspire in the Moslem hope, peace, courage, virtue, and faith. Currently, however, its outreach is thwarted by complacency and pretension, its instrumentalities dulled for the lack of discipline in the principles of modern education. Every intelligent Moslem looks up to al-Azhar, he continued, as that seminary which should set the intellectual-spiritual pace. From its halls trained men, fit to lead the community in truth and reformation, are expected. But the bitter fact is that an Azharite preacher is not understood save by those of medieval mind. A source of contradiction is thus discovered in the Azharite's inability to preach a living faith, and in the failure of the educated classes to find spiritual sustenance at the hands of reactionary leaders.

Another illustration of this contradiction may be cited. It relates to the tension that exists between freedom and authority. Modern Turkey illustrates what happens when an Islamic state turns to Western secularism. The immediate result was impatience with Islamic faith and culture, ostensibly without repudiation, however, of either in essence. Turkey broke off with the outward symbols of Islam such as the fez, veil, Friday as day of rest, and the Arabic alphabet. Devotion, religion, and true piety were not to be abandoned, however. Outwardly at least, belief in Allah and his rule over the destiny of men and nations was not in jeopardy. Evidence shows that Ataturk is not being currently sketched as enemy of true religion.

Yet few who have intimate knowledge of contemporary Turkey would venture to say that that state has resolved the deadlock between the authority of religion and the freedom of a secular government to organize life. This contradiction touches a profound and inevitable issue. It is the contradiction encountered by a secular state that arrogates to itself the right to order human destiny. In placing its edicts above divine ordinances, such a state promotes an idolatry rendered more venal by the emergence of the belief that man has freedom to manipulate spiritual affairs.

2. *The Recalcitrance of Modern Islam.* Behind the recalcitrance of modern Islam are its volatile protestations against injustice and its repugnance to highhanded control, especially if engineered from the West. This is a complex of repressed and pent-up emotion, partly the residue of millennia of East-West hostility. In short, the recalcitrance of Islamic peoples can hardly be detached from that of Christendom.

That modern Moslems have been quite unable to circumvent this historic enmity is fully attested in their thought, feeling, and literature. Whether the generality of Christians have or have not been able to circumvent it is equally open to doubt. This is a matter inherent in the eternal character of Christian-Islamic relations.

The magnitude of what is here at stake involves the whole pattern of world peace and the urgent necessity to organize the world community. Mohammed Abdullah Enan wrote a popular treatise, *Decisive Moments in the History of Islam,* geared to the proposition that the encounter between Islam and Christendom in war and peace was always decisive and far-reaching in effect upon their destinies. Some have seen in the Islamic-Christian conflict a parallel to that between Communism and the West. Such an analogy, despite certain external similarities, is as misleading as it is untrue. It would be utterly false to say that Islamic recalcitrance is invariably poised to strike against the West. Nor is Islam constantly engaged in an existential struggle aiming at the elimination of Christianity.

In our time, the West must be held equally responsible with the Middle East for the kind of Islamic recalcitrance with which everyone is familiar. Sati al-Husari, an exponent of Arab nationalism, wrote an essay on the short-lived reign of King Feisal in Damascus. Under the title " The Day of Maysalun," he gave a report on the military engagement of July 24, 1920, when the troops of General Gouraud dispersed the Arab defenders of Syria. In the destruction of the first Arab state of modern times, al-Husari saw the opening round in a struggle which lasted a quarter century, ending in the ultimate withdrawal of France from the Levant. Ranged against each other throughout that period were the forces of the Arabs and the military might of the Third French Republic.

In a larger sense, deterioration fouls the contacts of Islamic states with their neighbors. Whether the adversary happens to be Hindu, Zionist, Communist, imperialist, or quite ironically a fellow Moslem, the end result is a melancholy blow to internal stability and a day-to-day foundering in international affairs.

3. *The Nature of Ultimate Reality.* This analysis would be incomplete if it did not touch upon the Islamic view of ultimate reality and the nature of man. This is in order if only because the conception of ultimacy and manhood has a direct bearing on the structure of a religious tradition.

In *A Pilgrim in Arabia,* H. St. John B. Philby, the renowned British convert to Islam, speaks of the fear which King ibn-Saud inspired among his subjects as a derivation from the fear of Allah. The fear of the monarch, he says, is but a natural extension of that fear of God which is the basis of Islam. Yet Mr. Philby did observe that the Wahabi subjects of the late Saudi king scarcely drew the right distinction between a God who is manifestly infallible and therefore to be feared, and fallible monarchs who need the advice and control of their subjects. What, then, according to the Islamic religious tradition, is the proper understanding of ultimate Reality, that is, God?

The reader will recall the positive theological faith of the Moslem already discussed in this chapter. Suffice it to say at this point that the words of the Islamic confession, which declare that there is no deity save Allah, in effect impose a limit upon man's knowledge of God. The conception of God in Islam obviously centers in that kind of mystery which bars access to the Eternal. Allah is Absence, a God ever hiding himself. Even the man of deepest faith may not aspire to draw nigh unto the throne of grace. Hence, it is not given the believer to approach Ultimate Reality and, being transformed, to bear witness to the Eternal. Nor is orthodox Islamic doctrine fruitfully concerned with the mystery of Allah. The faithful seeker is not enjoined to make an encounter with him. An Eternal, remote from human comprehension, an absolute stranger to mortal expression, would not be likely to disclose himself, much less wrestle with mortal man.

Mohammed Abduh stands without peer in modern Islamic thought. As regards all that relates to the dogma of God, his essence and attributes, Abduh's circumspection was truly phenomenal. With meticulous insistence, in his *Epistle on the Unity of God* and elsewhere, Abduh counseled his disciples that they should remember where to stop in their contemplation of Divine Reality. Reason has a boundary that may not be transgressed with impunity, declared Abduh. By this he meant that the faith could not be defended if intellectualism exceeded its bounds. Only such a curb upon thought, in his opinion, could protect a strategic retreat to the position where the historic mystery of God was affirmed as final. Castled in al-Azhar, this modern Islamic theology abides a captive to the concept of the ineffable Allah.

4. *The Islamic Conception of Man.* Generally speaking, Islam viewed man as a microcosm, reflecting the cosmos in its

entirety. Man was ruled by the gift of reason which Divine Wisdom bestowed. Yet opinion was divided as to what constituted human nature. Some contended that each person was born with a set, unchangeable character. Others held that education and training were sufficient to produce piety. Others still thought that inherited bias could be reduced through discipline. In its final classical stage, Islamic orthodoxy seemed agreed that man had two spirits. One of these died with the body. The other, an "atom," which although a substance yet was not fundamentally corporeal but rather breathed into man by God, was therefore destined to everlasting life.

The core of man's being was deemed to consist in his knowledge of the Eternal and the ultrasensory realm. But the nature of God being absolutely hidden, as we have just seen, the true nature of man likewise remained a mystery. To be sure, Islam delivered man and woman from promiscuity through strict marriage legislation. But the status of woman was left vague precisely because the status of man was vague; and their common manhood lacked specific definition as a basis for equality. Nor was the situation clarified when ontology with its emphasis on existence and being agitated the minds of philosophers struggling with Greek concepts. Even less conducive to a basic settlement was that notion of union with God which the Sufi mystics introduced. Incidentally, their case was not helped by reaction against Koranic transcendentalism or by their gleanings in foreign cultures and non-Islamic patterns of devotion.

The immediacy of God and the dignity of man did not lead to spiritual intercourse between Creator and creature. Both man and his spirit were regarded as accidents: man, because all that is made by Allah is subject to an arbitrariness that was felt even though not explicitly posited; his spirit, because the spirit was life other than the soul. God alone created man's acts, even the bowing and prostration of worship. The rationalist affirmation of free will jarred the orthodox believers, who rested all articulation in the effective dynamism of Allah without recourse to secondary causes. The paradox of God's absolute power and freedom, on the one hand, and man's freedom of will and action, on the other, was side-stepped before the tide of controversy had subsided.

That is not to say that modern Moslems take kindly to the strict postulations of medieval religion. A rationalist upsurge is detectable in Pakistan and Egypt. Nevertheless, the true meaning of manhood has been shrouded by an overlay of anthropocentrism which obscures both the inscrutability of Allah and the possibility of human transformation. Divided by a dual allegiance, to its own theological patrimony and to Western ideas, modern Islam has yet to contribute to the resolution of inner tensions. What is man? Is he free or determined, free and determined, neither free nor determined? Is it possible to comprehend the meaning of modern history, existence as such, the destiny of individuals and nations, and the structure of life apart from concern with man himself? Dare we ignore the flood of light which the science of psychology has thrown upon personality, and still claim to know the truth about man?

If the Middle East cannot be understood apart from Islam, neither can that religion enkindle spiritual vitality without due regard to its peoples' needs and hungers. But a truly reformed Islamic tradition might yet bring greater unity and tranquillity of soul to the region as well as encourage more fruitful relations abroad.

4

THE EASTERN CHURCHES: ORIGINS

ANTECEDENCE and continuity suggest themselves as key words which promise to open up the rich and hallowed heritage of Middle East Christianity. Antecedence in relation to our theme essentially means that the Christians were there centuries before Islam. As for continuity, it means that in contrast to the once brilliant record of the region's Judaism, Christianity in this setting justly claims a superior degree of mobility. This is evidenced by the fraternal participation of Christians in indigenous affairs and in the evolution of social as well as political consciousness.

To stress this point is by no means to overlook the singular and once resplendent contributions of either Islam or Judaism. Quite the contrary, it is generally conceded here that adherents of the two other great religions do bring to their twentieth century tasks a fund of tried and tested values. These are sorely needed in an epoch that imperatively calls upon men everywhere to co-ordinate their faith in freedom and world peace, and to discharge their responsibilities in the light of the races' cumulative wisdom.

It is nonetheless true that Christianity in keeping with its genius has earned for itself an admirable position in the region's culture. Although alternately fraught with divisions and exposed and jettisoned, the Eastern Churches have by a strangely benign providence contrived to come through seared yet radiant, outnumbered but confidently buoyant and chastened. Representing minority groups in most of these lands, Christians number an estimated seven million, unevenly distributed in a regional population of some one hundred and ten million. In states that extend from Egypt to Iran and from Turkey to Ethiopia, Christians constitute a resilient demographic element. They have recurrently shown an astounding will to meet crises with tremendous resources of courage and vitality.

That is partly the reason why the Eastern Churches have earned a certain right to serious consideration in a treatment that aspires to depict the Middle East in religion and culture. Theirs is an ancient role and inspiring epic which cannot be swiftly disposed of or sweepingly written off. In direct and incessant contact with Europe and Asia, America and Africa, they hold a stake in such matters as religious liberty and the intrinsic dignity of man. The achievement of a firmer international order is one of their perennial concerns.

Beginnings

At the center of the storm that raged within the old Church, tearing apart the several bodies of Middle East communions and aggravating already existing cleavages, was an inalienable curiosity. The mind was tempted to prove the inscrutable mystery of the cross and to explore the hidden depths of the Lord's identity. Beyond the creedal divergences that emerged, and the confessional barrier walls soon to be erected, stood the pride of theologians. Intent upon scoring an intellectual victory, they deliberately laid the blessed Redeemer, so to speak, on the dissecting table. Few were in distress even if they should squander the precious gift of One who entered the world in order that he might be the object of man's affection and adoration. The cause of idle scrutiny, interminable speculation, and disputation, seemed central.

In the polemical investigations that were staged, the harmonizing presence of the Prince of Peace was all but forgotten. The vital spirit of Christian love and fellowship failed to assert itself in the midst of those whose prudence and com-

petent erudition otherwise left little to be desired. When finally construed, the settlements were not the outcome of calm
inquiry and mature judgment. They came out of a frenzied
arena where cleric quarreled with cleric, and where the loosing
of religious passion had transpired in a series of clashes between metropolitans, bishops, and patriarchs. The overtones
soon became rivalries and rifts, estrangement between ecclesiastical prelates, noisy councils, imperial edicts, exiles, riots,
and schisms.

Such were the inner moods and circumstances encompass-
ing the central stage where Greek theology wrangled over the
dogma of the incarnation. From the pen of the Roman Catholic French historian Louis Marie Olivier Duchesne (1843–
1922), writing in *Histoire ancienne de l'église,* comes a terse
evaluation of what happened:

" We see at the end of the story the Eastern Church incurably
divided, the Christian empire broken up, the successors of Mohammed crushing . . . Syria and Egypt. This was the price of those
metaphysical exercises." (Vol. III, p. 324, Fontemoing et Cie, Paris.)

Now, then, the indigenous Christianity of the Middle East
originated undoubtedly in the labors of the apostles and had
no foundation other than that which the Master himself had
laid. The setting of its distinctively local types, however, was
intimately bound up with the momentous events that rocked
the Church and culminated in the condemnation of Nestorianism at Ephesus in A.D. 431.

Behind were the decisive Christological controversies of the
fourth century. The theological formulations climaxed at Ni-
caea (325), in the declaration that the Son is coessential with
the Father, and at Constantinople (381), in the assertion of the
deity of the Holy Spirit, had defined the doctrine of the Trin-
ity with penetrating insight and meticulous precision. All future
lines of approach to the subject had to fit into the Nicene-
Constantinopolitan framework. Within the theological determination of this creed there was ample room, however, for

further disagreement. To be more specific, new divergences might occur if the mind pursued either of these two courses: (1) that which threw into bold relief the distinction between the human and divine nature of Christ; (2) that which dwelt on the absolute unity of his person.

Emphasis on the distinction between the two natures came to the surface in Nestorianism. Insistence on the unity of the Lord's person led to the heresy commonly designated as Monophysitism, or better still Eutychianism, after the heresiarch of Constantinople, Eutyches (c. 375–c. 452). Deeper motivation still agitated the rival schools and shaped their discordant philosophies. In so far as Nestorianism was concerned, there was a veritable obsession with the humanity of Jesus. His earthly advent and ministry, his brotherly and filial relations, indeed his vernacular and ethnic kinship with Middle East folk rendered irrepressible the inclination of some to claim him as one of themselves. Prompting the Eutychian view, on the other hand, was the aim to exalt the deity of Christ. Consequently it appeared that his humanity not only would be eclipsed but virtually absorbed in all-pervading divinity.

In the upshot, this antithesis in the doctrinal orientation of the then contemporary theology came to be focalized in two cities, Antioch and Alexandria. They had long battled over the leadership of religious thought in a contest that often proved more dramatic than praiseworthy. Antioch drew its vigor in the bitter debate from an unbending commitment to the integrity of the Lord's human nature. Alexandria staked its prestige in the theological field on the touchstone of the overarching role of the divine nature.

There is no city whose name is more redolent in Christian annals than Antioch, ancient capital of Syria ceded by France to Turkey in 1939. Antioch was scene of the labors of Paul and Barnabas, the place where Christians first received their name. Behind this city, birthplace of the missionary movement, towers to the south Mt. Casius, and not far off in the west rises the Amanus range. Before it flows the Orontes amidst a scenic

valley. It was on the southern left bank of this river, some fifteen miles above its Mediterranean estuary, that Seleucus
Nicator founded the city about 300 B.C., naming it after Anti-
ochus, his father.

Under the Romans, Antioch prospered and came to be
known as "Antioch the Beautiful," "Queen of the East," and
"the third metropolis of the Empire," that is, after Rome
and Alexandria. Here, in the school of Antioch, traditionally
committed to the historical study of the Gospels and the pronounced evaluation of Christ's earthly life, Nestorianism flourished. With the rise of the Byzantine (Eastern Roman) Empire, and the ascent of Constantinople to power (330–1453) as
capital, Antioch's splendor did not vanish. Its citizens were as
a rule on terms of friendly intercourse with "New Rome,"
entrenched itself, was dedicated to the defense of Christ's divinity. Founded by Alexander the Macedonian in the year
where the prestige of the Syrian city rarely suffered loss.

Alexandria, where the Eutychian opposition to Nestorianism
332 B.C., the city had acquired a polyglot population of Egyptians, Greeks, Jews, and Romans, among whom the Greek
language was the ordinary medium of understanding. The renowned museum and library, established by the Ptolemies, advanced Alexandria's fortunes in the cultural sphere of the ancient world. The fusion of Semitic and Greek thought came
to fruition in the Septuagint translation of the Hebrew Scriptures into Greek, probably at Alexandria in the third pre-
Christian century. Exegetes such as Philo, who initiated the
allegorical interpretation of the Bible, represented a Judaism
permeated by the Greek spirit.

In the early Christian era, Alexandria, retaining its primacy
in Greek learning, became the seat of a catechetical school for
the training of the clergy. Ranking Christian scholars and writers, such as Clement (c. 150–c. 220) and his pupil Origen
(c. 185–c. 254), enhanced its stature in Christendom. Clement
was the first Christian intellectual to bring the culture and
speculation of the Greeks to bear on the exposition of religious

truth, in the belief that Greek philosophy was the preparation of the Greek mind for Christ. Origen, the greatest and most prolific theologian of the ancient Church, with the possible exception of Augustine, formulated a system in opposition to Greek philosophy, though he himself owed much to the neo-Platonists and Gnostics. As a formidable bastion of the Church, Alexandria also claims a succession of bishops, the caliber of whom is best represented by Athanasius (296–373).

For its earliest precursors the Nestorian tradition goes back to two men in particular, Theodore of Mopsuestia (c. 350–428) and Diodore of Tarsus (d. c. 394). Diodore founded the Antiochian dogmatic school and was a chief opponent of a contemporary, Apollinaris (d. 390), bishop of Syrian Laodicea. In seeking to affirm the full deity of Jesus, Apollinaris taught that the person of the Lord is an ultimate union of a perfectly divine with an incomplete human nature. He was a theologian trained in Platonic philosophy, and in his approach to Christology resorted to the Platonic psychology of light. His theology was anathematized at the Council of Constantinople (381), and it seems that the remote origin of Nestorianism is to be discovered in the anti-Apollinarist zeal of Syria.

First a priest at Antioch, then bishop of Tarsus in Cilicia, Diodore was a famous defender of Nicene orthodoxy during the Arian controversy. Yet in discussing the union of the consubstantial Logos with the man Jesus, he evolved the core of Nestorian doctrine: that these are two persons, the Logos (Son of God) and the son of David; not the Logos, but the son of David, was born of Mary; the son of David was the temple of the Son of God; and the mystery of the incarnation consists in the assumption of the perfect man by the Logos.

As already noted, the school of Antioch where these ideas gained momentum also produced Theodore of Mopsuestia, another bold opponent of the Apollinarians, against whom he argued that for the restoration of the shattered unity of the cosmos it was necessary that God the Word should become perfect man.

In 392, Theodore became bishop of Mopsuestia, a small town in Cilicia about twenty-three miles east of Adana. He was a lifelong friend of that other great Antiochian, John Chrysostom. In the work of Theodore appear the ideas of Diodore, revolving about the theme that the man Jesus is only the temple of the indwelling Logos. Let it be said, however, that though the Nestorian Church, " Church of the East," regards Theodore with reverence as its chief doctor, the fact is that he died in communion with the Orthodox Church. A foremost exegete of Greek theology, he was a man of rare spiritual insight.

Reared in Antioch, where he had left his mark as a brilliant disciple of Theodore of Mopsuestia, Nestorius came to Constantinople in 428. Acclaimed for his beautiful voice, famed as a preacher, his already solid reputation had earned him appointment to the Imperial See upon the death of Sisinnius I (425–427) of Constantinople. The people for a while were highly elated on having secured from Antioch a second Chrysostom. It was not long, however, before the clash of Antiochian traditions with those of Alexandria precipitated the unhappy Nestorian issue.

The outbreak of theological hostilities had for immediate cause a denunciatory sermon preached by the presbyter Anastasius, a protégé of Nestorius. In the course of it the use of the title Theotokos ("Bearer" or "Mother" of God), as applied to the Virgin Mary, was bitterly attacked on the ground that she could not be said to be the mother of Christ's divine nature, but only of the human. That the title had long been in usage, and had received the sanction of Athanasius and others, did not seem to deter Anastasius or the patriarch Nestorius, who shielded him against the fury of the monks and the laity. As the storm gathered velocity, the opponents of Nestorius took their positions behind a platform epitomized in the words of Gregory of Nazianzus (d. 390):

" If anyone does not receive the holy Mary as Mother of God, he is separate from the Godhead." (*The Lesser Eastern Churches,* by Adrian Fortescue, p. 62, Catholic Truth Society, London.)

A test was thereby set by the so-called orthodox camp for belief in the Lord as one person. This tended to crystallize around Mary, making her the immediate object of the investigation. On the opposite side, the sermons preached by Nestorius reflected beyond any doubt the view that there were two distinct persons in Christ. They were the mere man Jesus, who was born of Mary, and the Word of God, who dwelt in him.

The man who rose to challenge Nestorius was Cyril (c. 376–444), patriarch of Alexandria. A churchman of outstanding intellectual qualities and attainments, possessed of an indomitable will, Cyril was less distinguished for personal integrity and the willingness to serve the cause of Church unity. In all fairness let us assume that Cyril regarded the term Theotokos as a safeguard of the Church's faith in the full deity of Christ. Yet the less disinterested motives ascribed to him are most devastating. Included among these are: jealousy for the power of his Alexandrian see and for his own prestige; anxiety lest Constantinople should come under the influence of Antioch rather than Alexandria; the desire to divert attention from accusations leveled at him personally; and even the ambition to secure such laurels in the new Christological disputes then in the offing as might buttress Alexandria against the rapidly growing primacy of Rome.

Toward his goals, Cyril took a number of steps in two directions: (1) that of fostering enmity against Nestorius in Constantinople; and (2) that of enlisting the support of Celestine I (422–432), bishop of Rome. The pope, though ostensibly steering clear of involvement in the East, decided in 430 that because the teaching of Nestorius was heretical, he must retract in ten days or be deposed. Delegated to carry out this sentence, Cyril, in a synod at Alexandria, drew up twelve anathemas against the Nestorian doctrine, of which the first declared:

"If anyone does not confess Immanuel to be truly God, and the holy Virgin therefore the bearer of God, for she bore according to the flesh, flesh which had become the Word of God, let him be anathema." (*Ibid.*, p. 63.)

Nestorius denounced these with twelve counter-anathemas of his own.

The controversy having reached these grave dimensions, Emperor Theodosius II (408–450) summoned a council, recognized as the third ecumenical, to meet at Ephesus in 431. Although the Syrian bishops, led by John of Antioch, did not arrive till a fortnight later, and the Roman legates later still, Cyril hastily convoked the assembly and insisted on proceeding with the stated agenda. Before so unrepresentative a council, for the most part composed of the Egyptian partisans of Cyril, Nestorius refused to appear and was condemned in absentia. Cyril himself, deposed by the Antiochian bishops who upon their arrival joined with Nestorius in forming a rival council, was nevertheless upheld by the Roman legates.

For the moment at least neither decision counted. But Emperor Theodosius, upon whom Nestorius hopefully relied, yielded in the end to powerful court intrigue. Banished first to Petra in Jordan, then to an oasis in Egypt, Nestorius finally died in exile about 451 at Panopolis. Hounded out of the Byzantine Empire, his followers carried with them the influence of his teaching and that of his more eminent teacher, Theodore of Mopsuestia, as propounded in the dynamic theological scholarship of Edessa.

The triumph of Monophysite theology as an exaggerated opposition to Nestorianism seemed assured. Publicly championed by orthodox leaders, it became generalized not only in Egypt, its historic stronghold, but throughout the Middle East. In its purest essence, this theology maintained that Christ had but one nature, that his humanity was so absorbed in divinity that he was scarcely to be reckoned as man. It is obvious why the ascendancy of such a doctrine could not long endure.

Dioscurus of Alexandria, Cyril's successor, craftily won a short-lived victory for the Monophysite cause at the eventually discredited Robber Synod of Ephesus in 449. The wrong was undone, however, in 451 at Chalcedon, when Dioscurus was exposed and the Monophysite doctrine condemned. This

Chalcedon assembly was the last of the four ecumenical councils recognized by both Roman Catholic and Eastern Orthodox Christians, as well as by most Protestants. Having first confirmed the positions of the three earlier councils, it proceeded to repudiate both Nestorianism and Eutychianism. In the settlement that was evolved, one reads:

" We, therefore, following the Holy Fathers, confess one and the same Son, our Lord Jesus Christ; and we do with one voice teach that he is perfect in Godhead and that he is perfect in manhood, being truly God and truly man; that he is of a reasonable soul and body, consubstantial with the Father as touching his Godhead, and consubstantial with us as touching his manhood . . . acknowledged to be in two natures without confusion, change, division, separation." (*The Greek and Eastern Churches,* by Walter F. Adeney, p. 101, Charles Scribner's Sons.)

This is the final orthodoxy to which Eastern and Western theology have ever since been committed.

Far from being thus silenced, however, the Monophysite party for nearly two and a half centuries continued to foment trouble. Widespread among such subjects of the Byzantine Empire as dwelt in the buffer territories separating it from the Sassanid Persian foe, the Monophysite doctrine loomed as a thorn in the imperial side. In a bid to his disgruntled subjects, Emperor Heraclius (610–641), seeking to alert them against the Arab-Islamic menace, proposed in 638 the Monothelete formula. This was a theological compromise devised by Sergius I (610–638), patriarch of Constantinople. Transcending the issue of the Lord's one or two natures, the formula took for its point of departure the theme that in him there was but one will, a single source of energy. An interim measure, Monotheletism was soon discarded, save for an extended popularity among the Maronites of Lebanon. They tenaciously professed it until the twelfth century, when they made peace with Rome.

Nor did the faith of Chalcedon, as touchstone of orthodoxy in classical Christianity, permanently guarantee the unity of the main Church. Already by the time of Photius (c. 820–

c. 891), patriarch of Constantinople, the papacy and Eastern Orthodoxy had drifted into a succession of estrangements ending in the separation of 1054 and the Great Eastern Schism of 1472.

In the meantime, the bulk of Syrian-Iraqi Monophysites had discovered in the person of Jacob Baradaeus (541–578) of Edessa a stanch champion. He was recognized in 563 as prelate of the Christian Arabs, and the Jacobite Church probably derives its name from his. Firmly rooted in Egypt, Monophysite theology, furthermore, annexed the Coptic Church and its Ethiopian affiliate. Having rejected the Chalcedonian decrees, the Armenian Church, in like manner, severed itself from Catholic Christendom. Provoked to unworthy ends by a series of events featuring dissension and withdrawal, Middle East Christianity then embarked upon a policy of organic isolation. Independent Monophysite communions took visible form in the lands stretching from Armenia to Ethiopia.

This rankling hostility was fanned into flame by the deeper feuds between the native populace and their Byzantine overlords. It played into the hands of the Moslem Arabs. Having acquired the Fertile Crescent and Egypt in the decade following the death of Mohammed (632), these intrepid conquerors lost little time in mobilizing the man power and resources of newly won provinces. This was intended for the more ambitious military operations planned against North Africa, Spain, and Asia Minor, as well as against Persia, India, and Central Asia.

COMMUNAL AND ETHNIC SURVIVAL

There is tangible evidence to show that in the Eastern Churches the historic faith provided the believers with a safety valve making for the preservation of communal and ethnic peculiarities. The survival among them of superstition and perversion must not, however, be charged against Christianity in direct contravention of its primary affirmations.

It would be well to lay emphasis on two points in this connection: that the forebears of the region's several Christian communities were the selfsame pagans to whom the first apostles addressed the gospel message; and that the expansion of Christianity was a slow process unfolding across the centuries. Emperor Constantine, on the thirteenth of July, 314, issued an imperial edict officially recognizing Christianity. Thereafter Christians acquired legal status and religious liberty. Yet certain proud cities of Palestine, such as Gaza and Ascalon, remained adamantly pagan.

The tide was yet to turn once more against the Christians. During the short-lived reaction that swept the Empire under Julian (361–363) the "Apostate," Christians were ravaged in the cities. A reversal of this policy occurred, of course, under Emperor Theodosius the Great (379–395). He enforced already existing laws that forbade magic, sacrifice to idols, and the obscene ceremonials indulged in at the temples.

But idolatry was too deeply ingrained to be so swiftly eradicated. The demolition of its shrines and symbols went on in many parts, at times in response to popular demand, at others in the face of violent local opposition. The riotous outbreak attendant upon the destruction of the Serapeum in Alexandria warrants the conclusion that the pagan spirit in the city was far from dead.

In his last edict, Theodosius ordered an Empire-wide closing of the temples and abolished the privileges of pagan priests. Paganism thereafter began to fade out. Gibbon spoke of its phenomenal disappearance as "the only example of the total extinction of an ancient and popular superstition." The fact of the matter is that paganism shed only its organism — its soul continued to brood over the familiar scene of the Bible world.

Both archaeological research and Middle East folk religion cast a shaft of light upon the nature of this defunct paganism and its superstitious survival. In *The Religions of Syria and Palestine* (1912), Frederick Jones Bliss, in line with the famed Chicago Biblical scholar, Samuel Ives Curtiss (1844–1904), affirmed the existence of a reasonable common ground of provincial religious practice between the popular forms of native Syrian Christianity, Islam, and Judaism. The cult of the shrines was a case in point. Veneration by Moslems of a saint known to them as al-Khidr (reminiscent of Greek Glaukos, the Green One, patron of mariners) had its counterpart in the Christian veneration of Saint George, and of Elijah by the local Jews. Partly to be explained as a derivative of the ancient cult of the "high places," this localized worship of saints and martyrs had more immediate affinities with pre- and post-Christian paganism.

The syncretic character of this paganism is endorsed by modern archaeology. Professor W. F. Albright leaves little doubt that the shrine worship of al-Khidr provides an example of the fusion of Greek and Aramaean religion. Archaeology verified that fact at Dura in Palestine and at Syrian Palmyra. The case rests on further evidence from Syrian and Nabataean temples, as well as on the inscriptional remains of paganism in the area. It appears that the full-bodied religion of Syria, between 300 B.C. and A.D. 500, was a syncretism reaching its height in the third Christian century. Reflecting this mixed Greco-Syrian religious culture is the Dionysiaca of Nonnus, a literary document dating from the fifth century of our era.

Cognizance of this communal and ethnic continuity is vital to the proper understanding of Christianity everywhere, and the Middle East is no exception to the rule. Yet if the saint worship of Syria-Palestine is of any significance at all, it must then follow that the paganism whose spirit encroached upon Christian history did not invariably reflect the genius of the ancient Orient alone. It was more directly related to the popular heathenism of the Mediterranean basin.

Confirmation of this is available, for example, in the case history of the well-known shrine of Afqah, dedicated to the Virgin Mother, on the Lebanese slopes north of Beirut at the source of the Ibrahim River. The pedigree of this Lady of Lebanon points back to Greco-Roman times. Celebrations, combining Semitic and Greek strains, in that period formed the basis of a cult that cast Ishtar in the role of a female deity who every spring when the river ran red mourned her slain husband Adonis.

In order the more specifically to portray the impact of that communal and ethnic tradition, suffice it here to fix attention on Syria. In its broad geographic and cultural connotation, this country has been from the beginning the nerve center of the region's Christianity. Its choice as a point of demonstration would be valid on the ground that Christianity itself is, humanly speaking, of Syrian provenance. The history of religion offers further justification of that choice. It stipulates that to grasp properly the meaning and intent of Christianity is to see its continuities and discontinuities with the other religious dynamisms of its early environment. Such dynamisms must include Judaism, Greco-Aramaic syncretism, and, subsequently, Islam, all observable at close range in Syria.

Such a procedure will inevitably prove the several religions involved, including Christianity, to be avid borrowers one from another. The latter faith at its core, however, only assimilated from others what may be described as "material" upon which the mark and genius of its extraordinary and unique interpretation was stamped.

To be sure, this Christianity had had its fierce battles with paganism, tyranny, and heresy. But until the fifth century councils of Ephesus (431) and Chalcedon (451), which saw the condemnation of Nestorianism and Monophysitism, Christianity had been relatively free from organic schism. Within the household of faith, it had a fairly homogeneous creed. Even when the Church was divided into patriarchates, sees, rites, and geographic-ethnic entities, it had remained generally one. It was upheld by a Roman Empire that could remain intact even though its central authority had been transferred to a Second Rome. There was at least the semblance of an ecclesiastical unity, rooted in the concept of the one, holy, catholic, orthodox, and apostolic Church.

Again falling back upon Syria as a point of demonstration,

we might observe that the growth of Christianity followed two parallel lines, two distinct streams of culture: Hellenistic in the cities, and Syriac-Aramaic-Semitic-Arab in the rural areas. In time, this differentiation gave birth to two types of Christianity, Greek-speaking Hellenistic and Syriac or Aramaic-speaking. Antioch drew attention as nucleus of the Hellenistic society, whereas Edessa similarly came to the forefront as focus of the more strictly indigenous Syriac community.

It may be argued that the principle of communal and ethnic stratification is, after all, an oversimplification of a historically complex situation and, at any rate, is ill-suited to Church history. Be that as it may, the aforenamed principle certainly gives us a clue to the subject in hand. It will prepare our minds for a fuller apprehension of the several traditions that constitute the totality of Middle East Christianity.

CHAPTER

5

FOUR CHRISTIAN TRADITIONS

THERE are accordingly four principal Christian traditions,
each inherent in a given heritage of communal and ethnic
character, that confront us in the Middle East. (1) There is the
Middle East ecclesiastical tradition proper. It asserted itself
when significant native constituencies made their exit from the
main Church upon the condemnation of Nestorian and Monophysite doctrines. (2) There is the Eastern Orthodox tradition. At first an integral part of the one Church, it was subsequently organized as independent patriarchates and Churches,
forming a major branch of Christendom. (3) The Roman
Catholic tradition resulted from the impact of the Latin West
and the establishment of self-governing national bodies. In
union with Rome and hence Uniat, these prefer to be known as
Catholics of Eastern Rite. (4) The Evangelical tradition took
shape as Americans and Northwestern Europeans carried the
message into the Middle East in the course of the nineteenth
and twentieth centuries. This Church of the Reformation gave
rise to ecumenically conscious native Protestant Churches.

We should now take up the four traditions in the above-
noted order.

1. *The Middle East Ecclesiastical Tradition Proper.* At first
glance it might strike one as quite arbitrary to recognize those
schismatics, pronounced heretical by the orthodoxy of the day,
as constituting the native ecclesiastical tradition rightly so-
called. Yet in keeping with the already considered principle of

73

communal and ethnic survival, both the Nestorian doctrine and its extreme Monophysite opposite were truly an expression of indigenous self-consciousness.

a. *The Nestorian Church.* Aubrey R. Vine offers in *The Nestorian Churches* a concise picture of this form of Christianity dating from the Persian schism to the modern Assyrians. Says he:

> "Nestorius . . . has provided a name for a heresy which he did not even hold, and for a Church which he did not found. . . . These [Nestorian] churches have never officially used the title Nestorian to describe themselves . . . ; their own designation is 'Church of the East.' The formation of these churches into a separate communion . . . reached completion when Babai (487–502), patriarch of Seleucia-Ctesiphon, declared that the churches which acknowledged him as spiritual head were henceforward to be completely independent of the churches of the Roman Empire and that Nestorian theology was to be the basis of their doctrine." (Pp. 21 f., Independent Press, Ltd., London.)

Three factors had contributed to the detachment of the Nestorian Church from the rest of Christendom. First, there was the attitude of the Sassanid Persian government, which favored in all Church affairs the primacy of the bishop of Seleucia-Ctesiphon. Secondly, there was the powerful personality of Barsumas, a churchman who sought the independence of his communion. Thirdly, the influx of Nestorians from Edessa had facilitated the Nestorianization of the Persian Church. For many years, the Persian clergy had been trained at Edessa and thoroughly understood the Nestorian viewpoint which eventually triumphed in their midst.

It may be said, therefore, that this Nestorian Church, whose modern heirs are the so-called Assyrians, arose not only as a monument to the awakening national consciousness, but also as an expression of a profound theological heart-searching. What the imperial and ecclesiastical authorities described as Nestorian and heretical was in reality a Church which fought valiantly for freedom in the truth. It did not tolerate the use of imagery and in its worship all pictures and paintings were barred. It was a Church with memories of wholesale martyrdom under Persian persecution and far-flung missionary enterprise. It contented itself with a plain cross as the chief symbol of its faith, laid over a simple church altar. When one recalls all that and also bears in mind the fact that the Nestorian Church once repudiated the celibacy of the clergy, he will perhaps appreciate why it has been described as the ancient " Protestantism " of the Middle East.

b. *The Coptic Church.* To the Monophysite communion belong the Copts of Egypt, whose Church also arose in response to national sentiment. For fifteen centuries it guarded the faith against the odds of arrogant rulers and recurrent persecution. Indeed, from the time the Egyptian Monophysites organized their separate Church, after the Council of Chalcedon (451), till the British occupation in 1882, this indigenous Middle East community had had little respite from anxiety.

In the first century of their separation, the Copts were subject to Byzantine pressure aimed at forcing their acceptance of Chalcedonian orthodoxy. The interludes of this tyranny were the brief spells when the Coptic authorities wrested the upper hand and began to retaliate in kind against their foes.

Then in 639 the Arab conquest of Egypt launched an Islamic regime which persists to the present day. The line of Coptic patriarchs continues to run unbroken side by side with that of their Chalcedonian rivals. Even though the Arabs were not, and are not, notorious for religious bigotry, the historic truth is that in Egypt the adherents of Christianity and Islam have not always been at peace in their common life. In short, the heritage of the Copt includes many a painful memory.

Across the dreary march of time, the Coptic clergy and laity managed to keep Christianity alive in their ancient land. Except for its liturgical use, Coptic, their original tongue, vanished and was ultimately supplanted by Arabic. Whether driven by fear or motivated by the desire to improve their social status, enormous numbers turned to Islam. But apostasy failed to lure them all. Greater than any scar that heresy might have caused them to carry were the wounds that the loyal remnant willingly endured for the prize of the high calling.

Confirmed Monophysites that they are, and shrinking at the very thought of Chalcedon, the Copts repudiate nevertheless both Eutyches and Nestorius, boasting an orthodoxy of their own. At the Elevation, that is, when the priest raises the just-consecrated Eucharistic elements for the people to behold, he hails

" the body and blood of Immanuel our God. . . . This is the quickening flesh which thine only begotten Son our Lord and our God and our Saviour Jesus Christ took of the Lady of us all, the holy Theotokos Saint Mary; he made it one with his Godhead without confusion and without mixture and without alteration. Having confessed the good confession before Pontius Pilate, he gave it also for us on the holy tree of the cross by his own will himself for us all. I verily believe that his Godhead was not severed from his manhood for one moment nor for the twinkling of an eye." (Slightly reworded form in *The Rites of Eastern Christendom*, by A. A. King, pp. 473 f., Catholic Book Agency, Rome.)

As of 1927, the Rev. B. J. Kidd of Oxford reported in *The Church of Eastern Christendom* that " both the hierarchy and the number of Copts in Egypt are much reduced," that is, in comparison with ancient times. He went on to say:

" There is now a Coptic patriarch at Cairo with twelve suffragans in Egypt and one at Khartoum. Their flocks are a community of about 667,000. Some are wealthy; and the majority are better educated than the mass of their fellow countrymen. Though they form only six per cent of the population, seventeen per cent of the children at school are Copts." (Pp. 445 f., The Faith Press, London.)

Actually, the Copts have maintained their proportion since the Middle Ages, increasing in number with the modern increase of population. Headed by the patriarch, the Coptic hierarchy has the usual orders with a special rank — that of qummus — reserved for senior priests. Monasticism, of long duration in Egypt, is still represented by many monks and a few nuns. Largely through Protestant education, the previously low standard of culture among the clergy is steadily rising.

The Coptic Church prays to saints and for the dead; profound devotion is addressed to the Virgin Mary. Its chapels and worship form the object of immense historical and liturgical interest. With its Alexandrian customs, this Coptic tradition elicits certain features that are in part more archaic than those of the Byzantine rite. Read in Coptic, the liturgy, astir with Greek formulas, is attributed to Saint Mark. On most days, however, the great Eucharistic prayer — the anaphora corresponding to the Preface and the Canon of the Roman rite — is not in the original text but based on the Greek of Saint Basil.

This Church has a calendar of its own reckoned as of A.D. 284, the beginning of its "Age of Martyrs." Like other Eastern Christians, the Copts observe their fast in a manner strange to a Roman Catholic since it involves a simple diet forbidding animal products. Eggs, milk, and butter are not used, and olive oil is substituted for animal fats.

c. *The Ethiopian Church.* To this same story of communal and ethnic survival belongs also the Church of Ethiopia which has remained comparatively unscathed since its inception in the first half of the fourth century. With all the moving pageantry of its tradition, this Christian community claiming a membership of about 3,875,000, according to the 1950 figures, persists as a living link with the days when the Romans ruled both West and East.

Tradition has it that the communication of the gospel first took place on Ethiopian soil with the advent of the Syrian Saint Frumentius (c. 300–360). Eventually, Frumentius received in 326 an appointment as bishop of Aksum from Athanasius of Alexandria. Thus began an association between the Church of Ethiopia and that of Egypt which has persisted into the twentieth century. In the more recent past, however, the sovereigns and clergy at Addis Ababa have been restive under the arrangement whereby their Church received a Coptic monk as primate. When the last vacancy in the top office of the Ethiopian Church occurred, the first native abuna, Basileos, was elected and duly installed in December, 1950.

The continuity of this separatist Church remained unbroken until the period 1550–1650 when the country came under Portuguese supremacy and the national Church, pressed into union with Rome, virtually became Uniat. Likewise in 1935, Mussolini's invasion threatened the Church of the land, severed its tie with the Coptic Church, and permitted the attempt to extend papal authority over it. The Ethiopian ecclesiastical tradition otherwise has held intact. Based on the Alexandrian rite, its liturgy has been consistently distinctive in that it is celebrated in Geez, an Ethiopian dialect and a cognate of Amharic.

Relatively less modern in outlook than most other Middle East Christians, the Ethiopians retain a greater variety of pagan superstition. They, moreover, Judaize in several matters such as the expression of deep reverence before an ark housed in every church. Ostensibly made on the order of the " original " Ark of the Covenant, it is preserved at the Cathedral of Aksum, their ancient capital. Beyond the sobriquet " Negush Negashti " (King of Kings), the emperor enjoys the dignity of the fanciful epithet " Lion of the Tribe of Judah " and claims descent from King Solomon and the Queen of Sheba.

Located in the Horn of Africa and on the shores of the Red Sea, Ethiopia has profound historical ties with the rest of the Middle East as well as with Africa. Enjoying a secure position on the high plateau of East Africa, protected by the Red Sea and its mountain fastnesses, the country has provided a permanent home for Christianity.

Ethiopian culture is a blend of the original African with Hamitic and Semitic strains. Amharic, the official language, is intimately related to Hebrew and Arabic. With this in mind, Haile Selassie I, emperor of Ethiopia, in an address to the United States Congress on May 28, 1954, recalled that one of his medieval predecessors was known as " he who maintains order between the Christians and the Moslems." The emperor also drew in broad outline a picture of the significance of Ethiopian Christianity:

" The two Americas and the continent of Europe together constitute exactly one third of the land masses of the world. It is in this one third that are concentrated the peoples of the Christian faith. With but rare exceptions Christianity does not extend beyond the confines of the Mediterranean. Here I find it significant that, in point of fact, in this remaining two thirds of the earth's surface, Ethiopia is the state having the largest Christian population and is by far the largest Christian state in the Middle East." (*The New York Times,* May 29, 1954.)

d. *The Syriac Jacobite Church.* In 543, Empress Theodora reversed the imperial Church policy and recognized Jacobus Baradaeus as titular bishop of Edessa and leader of the Syrian Monophysites. She thereby launched a powerful communion whose missionary exploits form part of Christianity's eastward expansion. Thus officially sanctioned, the Syrian Monophysites came to be known as Jacobites, after Baradaeus, their indefatigable organizer. As a Syriac-speaking community, they naturally utilized their vernacular in worship and in the production of Christian literature.

Four things about this Syriac Jacobite Church need to be borne in mind. First, that as a Monophysite community, it shared in an ecclesiastical communion, an international Middle East network, joining Copt and Ethiopian, Syrian, Arab, Iraqi, and Iranian, as well as Armenian. Secondly, that this Church embodied in itself the spirit of revolt against Greek and Roman institutions. Thirdly, that, being Syriac, this Church had vital connections with its rival, the Church of the East miscalled Nestorian. Fourthly, that although traditionally anti-Hellenistic and anti-Western, the Jacobite Church, like the Nestorian, produced a galaxy of scholars who took a profound interest in the study of Greek language and literature. Rooted in the rite of Antioch and based upon Syria, the Jacobite Church set up the bulwark of Monophysite doctrine in the western part of the Fertile Crescent as the Nestorians had secured their position farther east.

Of the several storied monasteries where this Church held high the torch of learning and piety, Dair al-Zafaran in the vicinity of Mardin, Turkey, became its leading see during the pontificate of Michael I the Syrian (1166–1199), an illustrious churchman and chronicler. Today the majority of Middle East Jacobites are citizens of Iraq, and only about one fifth of them are of Syrian nationality.

The primary gift of the Jacobites to Christianity undoubtedly was the Peshitta. Completed by Rabbulas, bishop of Edessa, this Bible did not include the Apocrypha, but consisted of the whole Old Testament and the New Testament except Revelation, II Peter, II and III John, and Jude. The standard version of the Syriac Churches, Nestorian and Jacobite alike, the Peshitta (literally, " simple ") gave the common people of Syriac speech what Jerome had offered the Latins, and has been aptly described as the Vulgate of the East. Several other versions and revisions subsequently appeared reflecting the studies and theology of Jacobite divines.

Taking all this literary and evangelistic vigor into account, Walter F. Adeney wrote in *The Greek and Eastern Churches:*

" From these facts we may draw two instructive inferences. First, if there was something particularly stimulating to missionary enthusiasm and promising for its fruitfulness in Nestorianism . . . , its extreme opposite was not excluded from the evangelistic mission. Second, while both Nestorianism, on the one hand, and Monophysitism, on the other, were anathematized by the Orthodox Church, and the leading supporters of both heresies excommunicated, the mighty spirit of the gospel, which is larger than all sects and creeds, was working through them for the extension of the Kingdom of God." (P. 50.)

Like the generality of Eastern clergy, the Jacobite wear gowns and heavy bowl-shaped hats. The priests shave their heads and grow beards. The bishops carry a staff topped with two serpents instead of the conventional miter and ring. The higher clergy are celibate whereas the lower may be married.

Consequent to the Turkish terror of the World War I epoch, the patriarchal see was moved to Hims, Syria. Severed from their home base in the Middle East by the Tartar invasions of the thirteenth and fourteenth centuries, the Malabar Nestorians aspired at solidarity with the Jacobite Church; but the transfer of allegiance was not consummated until 1665. The Jacobite patriarch now wields spiritual authority over some 365,000 believers in southwest India.

e. *The Jacobite Church of Malabar.* In its eastward thrust Middle East Christianity penetrated India. Conversions and intermarriage, particularly in and about Malabar, between resident traders and the native stock helped entrench its ecclesiastical orders. Starting from Iran, this type of Christianity had trekked into northern India. Also emanating from Iraq and the Persian Gulf and Arabian ports, it reached southern India and Ceylon by sea. Though shrouded in obscurity, those early beginnings unmistakably point to a Persian-Iraqi Christianity of the Syriac variety.

With such Syriac traditions and memories, the ancient Christianity of India rightly claims a record traceable to the fourth century. Known as "Christians of Saint Thomas," however, its members consider the apostle by that name as the founder of their communion, resting the case for their first century origin on this somewhat dubious contention.

The use of Syriac liturgy added to their peculiar Middle East religious background entitled members of this communion to be called "Syrians." As far back as the seventh century, they had a hierarchy under the jurisdiction of the Nestorian Catholicos of Ctesiphon. Anchored upon Iraq and Iran, this community shared the fortunes of other non-Arabs whose commerce stood to suffer upon the rise of Islamic power. Yet in the eighth and ninth centuries, Christians from Baghdad and the Islamic Middle East continued to reinforce the community of the faithful in Malabar. It attained such an international stature that King Alfred of England saw fit to dispatch an embassy to India.

Nor was this historic continuity seriously jeopardized in the sixteenth century when the Portuguese appeared on the Indian scene. Whatever racial affinities with the Middle East once existed had long disappeared, however, thanks to the integrating process inherent in the Indian ethos. Less conspicuously alien than the Parsees of Bombay, who are of Persian descent, the Christians of Malabar nevertheless currently maintain a deep consciousness of their Middle East Christian heritage. Internal rifts, however, have left them little scope for involvement in the old clash between Monophysite and Nestorian theologies. Indeed, no one seems to know whether this Indian Christianity was ever organically Nestorian or Jacobite. To be sure, the Nestorians were at one time in the ascendancy. But there is no conclusive answer to the question as to what influence the Jacobite minority exercised over the majority.

There is evidence to show that the two groups at times coalesced. The comparative ease, moreover, with which in later centuries members of the community became Jacobite or joined Rome is most revealing. One might be inclined to conceive of an earlier fluidity in Christian affiliation in that part of the world. The Mar Thoma Syriac Church of Malabar constitutes the Reformed Protestant-oriented wing of the Indian Jacobite community. Its metropolitan, Mar Thoma Juhannan, was a delegate to the World Council of Churches, held at Evanston, Illinois, in August, 1954.

f. *The Armenian Church.* Christianity may have had an earlier start in Armenia, as a tradition implies which credits Bartholomew and Thaddeus with the foundation of the country's Church. But the historic founder of Armenian Christianity was none other than a Parthian Armenian aristocrat, famed as Gregory the Illuminator. In A.D. 294 he was ordained bishop by the metropolitan of Caesarea in Cappadocia. He baptized King Tradt, and with that act the nation whose Church began as a mission field became the first to embrace Christianity officially as a body.

Such mass conversion, as elsewhere, meant the adoption of Christianity by a people who almost instinctively read into its

ecclesiastical structure elements of their pre-Christian heritage. It was no surprise, then, that the Armenians rejected the
Chalcedonian theology and espoused the Monophysite creed,
if only as a symbol of their political autonomy. Formalized by
Catholicos Nerses II at the Synod of Tovin (c. 554), this rupture with the main Church had been foreshadowed throughout the first half of the sixth century in anathemas against
Chalcedon heard at several Armenian Church assemblies.

Leon Arpee in *The Armenian Awakening* (1909) attempted
a sketch of his people's Christianity. Taking the period 1820–
1860 as the crucial stage of its modern revival, he depicted the
role that his countrymen performed in the regeneration of contemporary Turkey. Mede and Persian, Roman and Byzantine,
Arab, Mongol, Turk, and Russian in turn exploited Armenia.
For a long time, the Persians and Romans fought over the territory, and the former proved themselves particularly cruel
masters. From the seventh century until its incorporation in
the U.S.S.R., this Transcaucasian country — Greater Armenia —
was, except for the period 1829–1917 when under imperial
Russia, in Moslem hands. Many of its inhabitants forsook their
homeland and, moving westward, formed in Cilicia, Asia
Minor, a settlement — Little Armenia — which from the eleventh to the fourteenth century became the hub of the national
Church and had the city of Sis as capital.

Numerically, the National Gregorian Church ranks as one
of the largest indigenous communions in the Middle East, and
the story of its modern upheaval is truly fascinating.

" Among a people like the Armenians," to quote Leon Arpee,
" whose literature grew up almost exclusively in monasteries, it will
not seem strange that the revival of learning also should originate
in monasteries. The Armenian revival of learning owes its inception
mainly to two monastic institutions, namely, the Great Hermitage
and the Convent of Armdol." (*The Armenian Awakening*, pp. 14 f.,
University of Chicago Press.)

Both convents arose early in the seventeenth century, the first
in Greater Armenia, the second in eastern Turkey.

Tragedy became synonymous with the word Armenian as

the Turkish atrocities unfolded. The Armenian massacres of 1890, 1893, 1895–1896, 1909, 1914–1919 are without parallel in the region's modern history. Whereas the pogroms of 1895–1909 had directed their force against two classes — the Gregorians and Protestants (the Uniats and the Eastern Orthodox having been shielded by France and Russia, respectively) — the slaughter of World War I, and after, spared no Armenian. The same policy of extermination devised by Talaat Bey and the Young Turks was pursued even more relentlessly by the Kemalist regime in and about 1920. In the process, the Armenians of Turkey were reportedly reduced from 1,800,000 in 1895 to 281,000 in 1922. Today an estimated 3,000,000 Armenians inhabit their ancient country in the Soviet Union or are scattered abroad. The Catholicos of Sis now resides in Lebanon.

Despite decimation and Communism, the Gregorian Church has not relaxed its witness nor has its creative role in the Middle East ceased.

2. *The Eastern Orthodox Tradition.* Not less indigenous is the Eastern Orthodox tradition. The Greek liturgy of this communion breathes the spirit of the Middle East and reflects the region's genius for serenity and devotion. An array of Greek Fathers and an impressive Byzantine heritage shed an aura of authenticity upon a Church of venerable stature in the annals of Christendom.

From the Byzantine Empire the Orthodox Church has derived the autocephalous form of Church polity. As a principle, autocephaly affirms it a self-evident axiom that where an independent state exists there is also to be an independent Church. Though free thereby from external authority, the self-governing Churches within Orthodoxy nevertheless maintain communion one with another and with the Ecumenical see of Constantinople.

Inextricably related to autocephalous government is another ecclesiastical phenomenon known as phyletism. It has marked the career of Orthodoxy, although attested elsewhere in the history of religions. Phyletism suggests racialism in Church affairs. It rests on the assumption that the jurisdiction of a national Church extends to all nationals and is not limited to those residing within the confines of the nation. In due course, that assumption won widespread approval and achieved doctrinal significance. With all its international and ecclesiastical implications, phyletism became a chronic source of trouble. In 1872 it was condemned by the Phanar (Ecumenical Patriarchate of Constantinople) in connection with the Bulgar schism.

Structurally, this Church is hierarchical. It holds that in the apostles our Lord laid the foundation of a hierarchy consisting of charismatic men. These united in themselves the gift of administering the sacraments together with prophecy and teaching. After the apostles, the communication of these gifts of the Holy Spirit became the special prerogative of the hierarchy, that is, the episcopate with its presbyters and deacons.

Thus the visible Church came to center about the bishops. Their office derived its powers from the apostolic succession, a divine institution of profound and holy meaning in Orthodoxy. Whereas parish priests may be men who upon ordination find themselves in the married estate, members of the higher clergy must be committed to celibacy. Other churchly features of Orthodoxy include the architectural design, which provides for the separation of the inner sanctuary by a screen. The celebration of Mass is a longer ceremony than that of the Roman Catholic liturgy. Except in those instances where a shift to the Gregorian calendar has been authorized, the Julian — thirteen days behind the former — is the general rule.

In the marriage ritual, the bride and groom are jubilantly crowned and march around the altar three times, performing other symbolic acts as well. Although the Roman Catholic Church, as we shall see, is quite influential in the Middle East, the majority of urban Christians in Syria, Lebanon, Palestine, and Jordan, and a host of those in Egypt, are Orthodox.

There are, all told, sixteen independent Orthodox Churches.

Of these, four are the historic patriarchates: Constantinople, Alexandria, Antioch, and Jerusalem. There are, next, three newer patriarchates, namely, those of Moscow (the Third Rome), Yugoslavia, and Rumania. Besides, there are the independent Churches of Cyprus, Sinai, and Greece.

The remaining six national Churches are: the exarchate of Bulgaria, the catholicate of Georgia, and the Churches of Poland, Albania, Finland, and Japan. Those Americans whose ethnic background reflects one or other of the Old World branches of Orthodoxy have instituted in the United States Churches of such origin as Russian, Greek, Yugoslav, Syrian, Rumanian, Bulgar, and Albanian.

As already noted, the several independent Churches of Orthodoxy are in communion with each other and with the Ecumenical Patriarchate of Constantinople. Although their basic rites are in Byzantine Greek, yet linguistic uniformity has not been a requisite. Where desired, the rite may be celebrated in the vernacular. Hence, Slavonic, Ukrainian, Rumanian, Georgian, Albanian, Estonian, Finnish, and Lettish are currently employed in the corresponding countries. Tartar in Siberia, Eskimo and Indian dialects in Alaska, Chinese and Japanese, and other tongues, have been accepted as vehicles of the liturgy. As might be surmised, the use of English in the American Orthodox Churches is on the increase.

Along with Greek, Arabic is common throughout the patriarchate of Antioch. The same is rapidly becoming true in the patriarchates of Alexandria and Jerusalem. Both Arabic and Greek endow Orthodox Christianity in the Middle East with a strikingly indigenous character. The denial of indulgence and purgatory by this communion is real. But it accords the veneration of icons an important place in its practice of piety. Sergius Bulgakov, the Russian Orthodox theologian, wrote in *The Orthodox Church:*

" The use of icons is based on the belief that God can be represented in man, who, since the Creation, possesses the *image of God* (Gen. 1:26), although obscured by original sin. God cannot be represented in his eternal being, but, in his revelation to man, he has an appearance, he can be described. Otherwise, the revelation of God cannot take place. The events of the earthly life of our Lord . . . are pictured in words in the Holy Gospel which, in this sense, is a verbal icon of Christ. . . . According to Orthodox belief, an icon is a place of the Gracious Presence. It is the place of the *appearance* of Christ, of the Virgin, of the saints, of all those represented by the icon, and hence it serves as a place for prayer to them." (P. 162, The Centenary Press, London.)

The crisis inflicted upon Orthodoxy by the Bolshevik Revolution is comparable with that other disaster of 1453 marking the capture of Constantinople by the Ottoman Turks. The Russian Church, greatest in wealth, numbers, and might, lay prostrate before the most determined antichrist of all time. Some of its doughty seers dared to believe, nonetheless, that it had been chosen to pass through a trial by fire in order to testify in spirit, in truth, and in liberty. The era of World War II, however, saw the establishment of a semblance of normal relations between the Soviet rulers and the patriarchate of Moscow. In the wake of the Revolution, sizable contingents of Russian exiles as well as such Orthodox hierarchies as those of Hungary, Poland, Czechoslovakia, and Finland had invoked the jurisdiction of Constantinople or otherwise sought the determination of their autonomy. International and geopolitical concerns eventually conspired to produce a bitter tension between the sees of Moscow and Constantinople.

When Alexis, patriarch of Moscow and all Russia, declared his intention to convoke a pan-Orthodox conference to meet in the Soviet capital, the patriarchate of Constantinople took exception. Its grounds were that it alone, as the Ecumenical see, had the right to call such an assembly. That conference did take place, however, in July, 1948. In attendance — other than the Russian representatives — were those of Alexandria, Antioch, Tiflis, Bulgaria, Bucharest, and Tirana. The delegates of Constantinople and the Church of Greece came to the jubilee celebration of the five hundredth anniversary of the autocephaly of the Russian Church. They did not participate in the concurrent conference, however, at which Moscow, they intimated, had usurped the historic right of Constantinople.

The Eastern Orthodox Church is steeped in a glorious tradition, immortalized by figures such as John Chrysostom and John of Damascus. In modern times it produced theologians of the rank of Bulgakov and Berdyaev, and valiant laymen such as Khomyakov and Solovyev. One of its most luminous votaries, in the second half of the twentieth century, is Dr. Charles H. Malik, the distinguished statesman and philosopher of Lebanon.

3. *The Roman Catholic Tradition.* The universal Church — for six hundred years after Chalcedon — remained organized in five distinct parts: the patriarchates of Rome, Constantinople, Alexandria, Antioch, and Jerusalem. Caesaro-papism, the subjection of religion to the state, first reared its head in Constantinople. To this phenomenon in ecclesiastical history, the Roman Catholic Church assigns the blame for Byzantine particularism and separatism. The trend toward a rupture between Eastern and Western Christendom — accelerated by Constantinople's new Turkish masters — finally became an accomplished fact in 1472. The Turks would not hear of the association of the Christian Church that had come under their sway with that of their Frankish foes.

For some time after, it appeared as though the Roman Catholic Church had washed its hands of the Middle East. The true specter of Christian disunity had long before loomed in the act of Pope Leo III, who on Christmas Day, A.D. 800, crowned Charlemagne emperor of the West. The Roman Catholic Church not only had broken off with Eastern Orthodoxy; it had withdrawn — or so it seemed — from the main stream of Middle East culture and religion. Yet largely through the efforts of Saint Anselm, archbishop of Canterbury, the Greeks of southern Italy and Sicily were consolidated with Rome at the Council of Bari in 1098. After the First Crusade, the Maronites of Syria-Lebanon, together with some of Asia Minor's Armenians, rendered tentative obedience to the pope.

The Roman Catholic tradition therefore was not completely barred from, or stripped of intervention in, indigenous Middle East affairs. On the contrary, the Holy See took pains to declare that the Church is catholic and not strictly Latin or European. Toward a more adequate exercise of responsibility in the region, several popes, as far back as Gregory III (731–741), had initiated policies which envisaged some sort of congregation or commission to deal with the spiritual problems of the region. Ultimately, in 1862, Pius IX instituted a Congregation for the Propagation of the Faith. Identification with the Propagation, whose primary concern was with the non-Christians, proved unsatisfactory. In 1917, therefore, Benedict XV set up a new and independent Sacred Congregation for the Eastern Church, a name later shortened into "Sacred Eastern Congregation."

Much of this interest was obviously traceable to the period of the Crusades, when Rome came into intimate contact with the Churches of Syria and the Middle East. The region, in the meantime, had been definitely envisaged in the steps taken by Pope Gregory XV in 1622 toward the consolidation of the Propaganda of the Faith. During the nineteenth century France subsidized the Society of Jesus in the region. It extended support to other orders such as the Christian Brothers. The pope had sent an apostolic delegate to Syria, and in 1847, the Latin patriarchate of Jerusalem created during the Crusades was re-established.

The chief centers of metropolitan life such as Beirut, Jerusalem, Damascus, Baghdad, Cairo, and Alexandria are today the scene of impressive Catholic activity, Latin cathedrals everywhere arising. The truth is that the Roman Catholic Church wields a gentle influence in most of the region, particularly Syria, Lebanon, Palestine, Iraq, and Egypt. Valiant efforts have resulted in the formation of indigenous churches united with Rome and hence called Uniat, or more accurately, Catholic of Eastern Rite.

In the first of two volumes, *The Christian Churches of the*

East, Donald Attwater details the precise relation of the Roman Catholic Church to Middle East Christianity:

" From the earliest times a primacy of the see of Saint Peter in Rome was recognized by all other sees, and the next most important bishops were those of Alexandria . . . and Antioch . . . , and these were also the three chief cities of the Roman Empire. After Constantine the Great had transferred his capital to the East, Constantinople soon climbed to the second place of ecclesiastical honor. These four cities give their names to the four chief types of Christian liturgy which with their variants are in use today. In the early centuries the East played a preponderating part in Christian history and thought. (Greek was the language of the Roman Church until about the middle of the third century; Latin was first used for liturgical purposes in Africa); the Greek fathers and doctors not merely left an ineffaceable mark but were the fundamental formative influences in the post-Apostolic Church; the first eight ecumenical councils were predominantly Oriental in their constitution. For seventy-five years in the sixth and seventh centuries almost every one of the popes of Rome was a Greek or a Syrian: and there were others; over twenty Oriental popes in all." (P. 3, Bruce Publishing Co.)

The present line-up of Catholics of Eastern Rite reveals that there are some eighteen different bodies. Thus, upholding the Byzantine Rite are (1) Bulgars, (2) Greeks, (3) Hungarians, (4) Italo-Greek-Albanians, (5) Melkites, (6) Rumanians, (7) Russians, (8) Ruthenians, and (9) Yugoslavs. In the so-called Chaldean Rite — consisting of former Nestorians or their offspring — are (10) the Chaldeans of the Middle East, and (11) the descendants of Malabar Nestorians. Out of the Armenian Rite came two bodies, (12) that of the Middle East, and (13) that of oversea emigrants. The Alexandrian Rite is represented by (14) Coptic Catholics and (15) Ethiopians. Finally, the Antiochian Rite is perpetuated in three bodies, (16) the so-called Syrians who withdrew from the Jacobite Church, (17) the Maronites of Lebanon, and (18) the offspring of Malabar Jacobites.

Owing to their historical and regional significance, two of these Catholic communities — the Melkites and the Maronites

(5 and 17, above) — deserve special notice and are hereunder treated separately as representatives of the whole family of Catholics of Eastern Rite.

THE MELKITE CHURCH

Some Middle East Christians chose in the midst of burning issues and regional as well as ethnic antipathy against imperial interference, to abide by the doctrinal rulings of Chalcedon. They had thereby affirmed allegiance to the main, universal, orthodox, catholic Church. From their countrymen they thereupon won the scornful epithet " Melkites," that is, " royalists " in league with the hated Byzantines.

The upshot was that the Chalcedonian cause, thanks to this native remnant, retained a foothold in the sees of Antioch, Alexandria, and Jerusalem. Or, to change the metaphor, it gained the services of a fifth column which, indigenous Middle Eastern though its members were, kept in close touch with a Byzantine Greek hierarchy that was still in communion with Rome. Partly of Greek descent, the members of this communion had not, however, until the early seventeenth century fully adjusted themselves to the displacement of Syriac by Greek in their church services.

Justification for the inclusion of the Melkite Church in this section devoted to the Roman Catholic tradition rests on the fact that although half of its constituency is Eastern Orthodox, the other half since 1724 has become Catholic of Eastern Rite. The latter is subject to a patriarch who divides his time between Egypt and Syria where most of his flock reside. To all practical intents and purposes, the Orthodox wing of this Church has abandoned the name " Melkite " to the Catholic wing.

The growth, reform, and prosperity of the Melkite Church — whose adherents in the United States are commonly known as Syrian Greek Catholics — date from the patriarchate of the illustrious Maximos III Mazlum (1833–1855). His notable achievements included the integration of the believers, in the Ottoman Empire and Egypt, under a unified jurisdiction, and

their attainment of an autonomous civil status recognized by
the Turkish authorities. Currently, the Melkite sees are Damascus (the patriarchal eparchy), Tyre, Aleppo, Bosra, and
the Hawran; Beirut, Hims, Akka, Sidon, Banias, Tripoli, Baal-
bek, Zahleh, and Jordan; also, Alexandria, Cairo, Khartoum,
and Jerusalem. In 1811, a seminary at Ain Traz, Lebanon, was
founded, which until 1899 was a bastion of Melkite theology.

More than 150,000 strong, the Melkites have imparted to the
Roman Catholic tradition an indigenous character in the Middle East. Their clergy have received training at the Byzantine
seminary of St. Anne in Jerusalem. Founded in the wake of the
Crimean War by the French White Fathers in 1882 under the
leadership of Cardinal Lavigerie, this institution has rendered
a remarkable service. A few aspirants pursue advanced study
at the Greek College in Rome. There are, besides, three Melkite monastic orders, two centered in Lebanon, at Mash-
musheh near Sidon and at Shweir, and the third in Aleppo.
These three congregations of monks have long constituted the
mainstay of Melkite spiritual vitality.

Under direct Western impetus, whether Italian or French,
the monastic institutions of the Melkites have been infused
with the Jesuit and Capuchin spirit, although their earlier constitution was modeled on that of the Maronite Antonians. Their
members engage in missionary activity and retreats. They su-
pervise a polyglot printing press and participate in parochial
tasks. The shortage of secular priests has opened to these Melkite Basilian monks throughout their history vast opportunities
in the service of parishes.

THE NATIONAL MARONITE CHURCH
OF LEBANON

The region's most impressive Uniat community undoubtedly
is the Maronite Church of Lebanon. It is united with Rome in
its entirety, and not merely in part as is the case in practically
all other instances where a segment of an Eastern communion
declared allegiance to the pope. This Church enjoys, nonethe-

less, an autonomous status. Proverbial has become the response of a Maronite mountaineer during the Turkish regime who, on being asked to name his sovereign replied, "The patriarch is our sultan." Rome's Maronite seminary, founded in 1584 by Gregory XIII, has been made famous by scholars such as Sionita, Ecchelensis, and, above all, Assemani, author of *Bibliotheca Orientalis*, an inestimable reference on the Eastern Churches.

When the third council of Constantinople (680) condemned the Monotheletic compromise sponsored by Heraclius, the Maronites indignantly refused to abandon that doctrine. They thereby acquired the title Mardites (rebels), in which they gloried. In 685, they closed their ranks and organized themselves as a separate body. Native apologists and ecclesiastical fathers of the Maronite tradition repudiate much of the historical verdict on the origin of their sect and the derivation of its name. They quite naturally maintain the continued orthodoxy of their ancient Church.

On this latter theological issue, however, corroborative evidence from Islamic and Eastern Christian sources bears out the reality of the Monotheletic episode in Maronite annals. As for their name, the uncritical Maronite theory is that it is derived from their patron saint Marun (Maron, Maro, d. c. 410), who presumably had established a monastery at the source of the Orontes, having gathered around him some three hundred and fifty monks. Critical research, however, tends to derive the name from a later Marun, who died in 707.

Native to Lebanon, with Semitic-Phoenician-Canaanite and other racial affinities common to the Syrian homeland, the Maronite community has proclivities of its own. These might be partly explained by such an ancestral strain — as the next three paragraphs disclose — which has entered also into the national composition and conditioned the making of Maronite character.

A people of undetermined origin, leading a semi-independent national life in the fastnesses of the Amanus range of Asia

Minor, the Jarajimah, as they are styled by the Arab writers, furnished irregular troops and proved a thorn in the side of the caliphate centered upon Damascus.

On the Arab-Byzantine border they formed — in the words of Theophanes — " a brass wall " protecting Asia Minor. About 666, their bands penetrated into the heart of Lebanon and became the nucleus around which many fugitives and malcontents gathered, among whom the Maronites evidently grouped themselves.

The Ommiad caliphs of Damascus, Muawiyah (661–680) and Abd-al-Malik (685–705), agreed to appease this troublesome element within their borders. Finally, the majority of the invaders evacuated Syria and settled in the inner provinces or on the coast of Asia Minor, where they became seafarers. Others remained and constituted one of the elements that entered into the making of what today is the Maronite community of Lebanon.

From the Crusades till World War II, the Maronites continued the friends of France in the Levant. In the year 1860, consequent upon the bloody conflict with the Druse community, they achieved an internationally guaranteed autonomy for Mt. Lebanon. According to the census of 1942, there were 318,211 Maronite citizens in Lebanon. Their colonists, settled throughout the world, swelled this figure by several hundred thousand. These oversea Lebanese include sizable communities in Egypt, the Americas, and elsewhere. Maronite ascendancy in the Republic of Lebanon arises not only from history but more realistically from the dynamism of the sect and the fact that it exceeds numerically every other religious denomination in the country.

The Maronite Church uses Syriac and Arabic in its liturgy. It has retained noncelibacy on the priestly level. When a priest dies he is carried to the tomb in a chair, enthroned as it were. Members of the clergy wear the usual black robes and small black hoods or round, turban-shaped hats.

4. *The Evangelical Tradition.* Although less than a century

and a half old, Protestantism in the Middle East is today a thriving tradition. Arab, Armenian, Persian, Assyrian, and Ethiopian are the integral parts of its indigenous character.

This tradition is alive in scores of congregations presided over by native pastors throughout most of the region. Such cities as Damascus, Aleppo, Hims, and Latakia; Jerusalem, Haifa, and Nazareth; Amman and Basra; Teheran and Tabriz; Istanbul, Alexandria, Port Said, Cairo, Assiut, Khartoum, and Addis Ababa; as well as Beirut, Tripoli, Sidon, and the adjacent centers of population in the Lebanon hills — to mention only the better-known place names — are studded with a network of evangelical Churches. Hospitals, orphanages, schools, institutes, colleges, and universities have arisen in response to the evangelical challenge.

Whatever basic affinity may have originally existed between the modern missionary enterprise and the medieval Crusades, in point of essential motivation, the two historical phenomena are really poles apart. The address of Pope Urban II delivered in Clermont, southeastern France, on November 26, 1095, has been described as "perhaps the most effective speech in history." Therein the pontiff urged the faithful to " enter upon the road to the Holy Sepulcher, wrest it from the wicked race, and subject it " to Christian arms.

In what sharp contrast were the farewell instructions of October 31, 1819, which Dr. Samuel M. Worcester, Secretary of the American Board, directed to Pliny Fisk (1792–1825) and Levi Parsons (1792–1822), Protestant pioneer missionaries to the Middle East, at the Old South Church, Boston.

"From the heights of the Holy Land and from Zion you will take an extended view of the widespread desolations and variegated scenes presenting themselves on every side to Christian sensibility: and will survey with earnest attention the various tribes and classes who dwell in that land, and in the surrounding countries. The two grand inquiries ever present to your minds will be: *What good can be done?* and, *By what means?* What can be done for the Jews? What for the Mohammedans? What for the Christians? What for the people of Palestine? What for those in Egypt, in Syria, in Persia, in Armenia, in other countries to which your inquiries may be extended? " (*Fifty-three Years in Syria*, Vol. I, by Henry H. Jessup, p. 29, Fleming H. Revell Co.)

Nor does the available data indicate that upon their first encounter with the region's Christian elements the missionaries had determined forthwith to launch a Protestant Church. Rather did the consensus of opinion among them seem to suggest that the already existing Christian traditions of Western Asia and North Africa possessed essential merit and validity and were therefore to suffice if reformed. Yet it was not long before the evangelical communion arose, taking concrete form in 1848 when the first Protestant Church was born.

Dr. John Wortabet (1827–1908), by virtue of his Armenian descent, Syrian birth, Arabic erudition, Scottish and American education, and his achievements as physician, scholar, professor, and theologian-missionary, may be regarded as the first and foremost ecumenical figure of Syria. He recorded, in *The Religions of Syria*, the legal recognition of the Protestants as a distinct and independent community within the Ottoman Empire:

" The first royal mandate to this effect was issued about the beginning of 1848, and since that time several imperial firmans [edicts] have been published, a civil head of Protestantism has been elected in Constantinople, and the privileges of the new community have become known throughout the empire. Persecution was thus the means of diffusing the Protestant name, and to some extent the distinctive doctrinal features of Protestant Christianity among a large number of people who would have otherwise remained ignorant of both." (P. 399, James Nisbet & Co., London.)

Conflicting reasons have been advanced to account for the emergence of this fledgling evangelical tradition. One ought, at any rate, to be content to think that, as elsewhere, the principal and pure motive did not consistently remain unalloyed. Our concern here is with Protestant missions and with the ecumenical movement at a focal point. Therefore we have addressed thought to the rise of evangelical Christianity in the region.

The infant tradition was the confluence of varied polities and strategies: In Palestine, Anglicans (Episcopalians) had planted the seed; in Syria-Lebanon, Presbyterians; in Egypt, United Presbyterians; in Asia Minor and European Turkey, Congregationalists. Other denominations had also laid the rising Protestant tide under heavy debt.

In bare essentials, the doctrinal platform of evangelical Christianity was easily explained. It struck the Pauline note that justification is by faith. Religion, that meant, was not merely a matter of good works. Direct access to the Eternal was possible and every believer had the right of private judgment. Freedom of conscience involved everyone's responsibility to rethink his faith. That salvation is by grace and through Christ meant the priesthood of all believers. Thus the foundation of an evangelical tradition was laid.

Clericalism, apostolic succession, hierarchical orders, and prelatical Church government came under heavy fire. Monasticism and formalism were sharply rebuked. The sanctity of the home and family, Bible-centered piety, and the fellowship of the redeemed took on new significance. Even if the evangelical leaven molded a tradition, yet in it was also the strong disposition to counteract the tendency to become ingrown.

Such a transformed Christianity, radiating through a tiny evangelical community, is upheld today by some 100,000 believers. Better orientation to Christians and non-Christians, as well as vital intercommunion with world Christianity, begin to evolve. Whether in the East-West struggle, or in such regional issues as the Arab-Israeli conflict, the evangelical tradition has important things to say. It holds the key to a more stable order on the national and international levels.

Finally, Christians of the Middle East, followers of the four traditions discussed, need be no one's clients. In close partnership with their Moslem countrymen, they do serve a high cause: the cause of religion and culture. In evil days, they stoutly endeavor to weave together at least a semblance of unity within their homeland and beyond.

6

RECORD OF JUDAISM

ONE ROOT of anti-Semitism (opposition to the Jew for what he is) lies buried deep in the soil of the Middle East, where in his first homeland the Hebrew distinguished himself and was set apart by his religion and law. There it was that his religious and national heritage had its inception. There Judaism's rich medieval effervescence took shape, and there the Dispersion ever fixed his gaze.

In a profound sense, therefore, always a thing apart, the Hebrew society which first arose in Canaan was nonetheless an integral part of Syria-Palestine. It formed a thin segment of that very literate Near East constituting the western fringes of the Fertile Crescent. That to this area went the credit for mediating an alphabetic script to the world was perhaps symbolic of a civilization within whose borders law, the basis of civilized society, was early set down and made public. Such a conception of law was endorsed by the Old Testament injunction, "Justice, and only justice, you shall follow, that you may live and inherit the land which the Lord your God gives you" (Deut. 16:20).

This type of law, as Dr. I. Mendelsohn ably pointed out in "Authority and Law in Canaan-Israel" (1954), meant both justice and righteousness. It provided a safeguard for the rights of the poor against the rapacity of the rich. It emphasized equality for all before the law, a kingship that was not above the law, and a piety which enjoined man to walk humbly with his God. Writes Mendelsohn:

" In this respect the Hebrew codes differ in the most striking manner from the Mesopotamian and Hittite codes which are entirely secular. Viewing the whole body of laws as it is embedded in the Pentateuch, it represents three layers: (1) religious laws traced back to Moses; (2) Canaanite civil law which the Hebrews adapted to their own need when they settled in Palestine; and (3) legal precedents established in various Hebrew law courts and transmitted generation after generation." (*Authority and Law in the Ancient Orient,* p. 32, American Oriental Society.)

Precisely that sets Judaism apart in the annals of the Middle East almost from the very dawn of the Hebrew tradition. In entering the land of ancient Israel we encounter a people radically different from their total environment in social heritage and spiritual outlook. Whereas elsewhere an aura of semi-divinity surrounds the royal personage, here among the Hebrews kingship was but an outgrowth of the office of judge. Set up in order to defend the country against foreign enemies, it lacked sanctity. Its only claim in the sphere of religion was to an approval reluctantly given by the spokesman of the Eternal.

That is not to say that the kings of Syria-Palestine were the wielders of naked autocracy. Royal authority was circumscribed by a state council whose members were recruited from the ranks of the rich agricultural and commercial families of city-states. Where in the Ugaritic texts the Keret legend reports that the king once invited his seventy " bulls " and eighty " gazelles," the judicious translator helpfully suggests that for the two words we read, respectively, " peers " and " barons." We should similarly understand Old Testament references such as Ex. 15:15; Isa. 14:9; Ezek. 17:13; 34:17; and Zech. 10:3, where " the oxen of Edom," " the rams of Moab," and " the he-goats of the land " are cited. In all probability, those were members of an aristocracy who shared with the king the powers of government.

Judged by their ancient record in the Middle East, the Hebrews, not unlike their immediate neighbors, were legal-minded. In keeping with their social and religious background, the citizen-king relationship was based on a solemn covenant.

A distinctive behavior pattern, however, held them apart from the Gentile world. The Babylonian Creation epic, for instance, affirmed that the gods had created man in order that he might provide them with food and shelter, he having started as a conditionally freed slave. But the Hebrew Scriptures maintained a directly opposite view. The book of Genesis declared man created in the divine image, and the psalmist (Ps. 8:5), varying the metaphor, said, "Yet thou hast made him little less than God, and dost crown him with glory and honor."

Of course we ought not to read a full-orbed democracy into the covenant order of ancient Israel. Nor is it to be assumed that the king was a kind of constitutional monarch held ac- the sacred texts occur such as " all Israel," " the men of Judah," or " all the tribes of Israel," one is well advised to accept such countable before the people for his acts. Where expressions in phrases as figurative. Or, these might refer to certain elders who represented the people, rather than to a popular mandate registering itself in an articulate national consciousness.

The weakness of the Hebrew monarchy was the price of that measure of freedom. The throne was also curbed by a system of checks and balances provided in the covenant. Indeed, an antimonarchical bias disturbed the entire history of kings. Kings had to contend with the very fact of prophecy, with its characteristic spectacle of inspired individuals rising in the city gates publicly to denounce the royal figure with impunity.

Inevitably, this sacred character of the law was bound to raise antipathy both at home and abroad. A political theory that suffered a king to rule restrained by the findings of an elders' council and the thunderings of a prophet and that upheld the concept of an essentially free citizen harbored the roots of trouble. At home, the outcome was a historic solidarity interrupted by defection and civil war, and an ethnic continuity disturbed now and then by monarchical instability.

Abroad, in Israel's multiple international relations, the record is frequently one of detachment and isolation. In sum, the Hebrews evoked among their neighbors the kind of negative response that flows out of jealousy and distaste for the unpredictable. And this elementary phase must enter into any serious review of critical factors behind anti-Semitism.

THE JEW AS A MIDDLE EASTERNER

From the first institution of the law down to Hitler's monstrosities, Judaism's decisive battles constitute the unparalleled epic of a people out of whose agony came the stanch prophets of old and their fulfiller, the Eternal Galilean. Thus in an Amos, a Micah, a Jeremiah, as in their peers, and in that Man of Nazareth, Judaism wrote out what to many is the strangest and most momentous chapter in the history of religion. And it all is the gift of a small, otherwise inconsequential people. On this central theme there can be little doubt.

The story of this amazing people, indeed the full drama of Judaism, may be told simply in terms of a holy vocation, of settlement in Palestine followed in due course by dispersion, then by a trenchant longing to return. Those movements into, from, and back to the Land are articulate with human pathos and divine instruction; they are fraught also with international, historical, and interfaith problems. As a rule, however, their importance and the controversy they incite by no means hinge on the bare events of settlement, migration, and resettlement. They are rather concealed in a round of religious, political, cultural, and universal involvements.

Suffice it by way of documentation at this point to interpret the Jewish role in the Middle East through the luminous career of Jeremiah who preached from about 623 to 586 B.C. A warning of imminent doom, his message was a summons to moral reform on the individual and national levels. In the face of political optimism, Jeremiah at the cost of grave personal danger lashed against priest and false prophet. Enough of a realist, he opposed resistance to Babylon, and his insistence on the unpopular truth earned him a term in jail. His stand against miscalculation in the international sphere was inspired by a call to penitence and humility.

Thus proclaiming eternal truth in time of peril, Jeremiah identified himself with the cause of his people. In their behalf he made intercession with the Eternal, the intensity of his prayer reaching the heights of integrity and faith. His was a faith in the righteousness of a God who will not forsake his own.

> " How can you say, ' We are wise,
>   and the law of the Lord is with us '?
> But, behold, the false pen of the scribes
>   has made it into a lie. . . ."
> We looked for peace, but no good came,
>   for a time of healing, but behold,
>   terror. . . .
> " The harvest is past, the summer is ended,
>   and we are not saved." . . .
> Is there no balm in Gilead?
> Is there no physician there?
> Why then has the health of the daughter
>   of my people
> not been restored?
>
> (Jer. 8:8, 15, 20, 22).

Yet nothing could be more inaccurate than to imagine that, steeped in its sacred legislation and prophetic vision, Judaism's ethnic insularity forbade the introduction of foreign ideas and cultural elements. Despite a proverbial rigidity, conservatism, and isolationism, the Jewish tradition, as evidence from different fields shows, is characterized by an amazing flexibility. Its conformity with novel conditions indeed seems phenomenal.

The field of religious art provides an apt example of Jewish hospitality to alien influence. Though somewhat overdrawn, *Jewish Symbols in the Greco-Roman Period,* by Erwin R. Goodenough, the Yale historian, demonstrates that Jewish art is impregnated with pagan importations. The use of Hellenized motifs abounds in the remains of Palestine graves as well as in the Jewish cemeteries of Rome.

In that part of the Middle East permeated by Roman political and cultural influence, religious symbols of a particularly Dionysiac type became a kind of aesthetic lingua franca. The artistic vocabulary remained essentially Dionysiac though expanded to encompass a variety of Oriental features. Among these were the Syrian solar eagle, rows of wine jars and baskets, the Egyptian waterfowl, and the Mesopotamian zodiac.

The fact remains that like the generality of Middle East peoples — Nabataeans, Syrians, Egyptians, and Anatolians — as well as others such as the Etruscans and Romans, the Jew was not absolutely immune to Hellenistic religious symbols. These he might have vigorously denounced, especially during Maccabean days, as tokens of rank idolatry. Yet with the passage of time and the changing mood his receptivity increased. Vitally moved by a strong allegiance to its own religious doctrine, Judaism tended to capitalize on those foreign symbols as proper means whereby man might more intimately approach the Eternal presence.

Having had this Greco-Roman culture to live with, Jews began to raise questions regarding their own inherited tradition, mindful of the comfort it brought on life's journey. Even those outwardly pagan forms and symbols, attested on Jewish tomb portals and synagogue façades, had a distinctively spiritual story to tell, true to the Hebrew norms of faith and hope. A stubborn persistence of " value " side by side with " alien form " may be surmised as the basic formula governing the Jewish adoption of foreign symbols. A tomb portal might thus serve as a mizrach ever pointing toward the east. A synagogue façade likewise will indicate God's quest for man. Passing through the threshold of a sanctuary, the worshiper treads the mystical path of communion with his Creator both now and forever.

A fresh breath of life came to Middle East Jewry as the seventh century rise of Islam inaugurated a creative phase of Arab culture and offered a setting for the wonders of medieval Jewish flowering. In *A History of the Jews,* Abram Leon Sachar, president of Brandeis University, states:

" Jewish religious life in these tranquil, unmolested centuries was governed by the Geonim, the heads of the famous academies. They were the spiritual descendants of the sages who had created the Talmud. They drew students from all over the world and trained them to carry unbroken the traditions which they had inherited. . . . One of the most important figures in the political and religious history of medieval Judaism was Saadia Joseph, who came like a bright star to light up the darkness of this age. In western Europe learning had almost completely decayed, and in the East Jewish intellectual life stood at a level only a little higher. Among Jews nothing of value, with the exception of certain midrashim, had been produced . . . since the time of Philo, who attempted to elaborate the doctrine of Judaism into a philosophy and to harmonize this system with the thought of the day. His work released a tradition of religious learning and speculation which vitally influenced his own and subsequent generations." (Pp. 161, 164 f., Alfred A. Knopf, Inc.)

Of Egyptian birth, Saadia (882–942) was a typical medieval Jewish scholar, equally at home in Arab culture as he was devoted to his own faith and people. Until quite recently, his true stature in medieval life had not been fully acknowledged. Mainly composed in Arabic, his works, after the closing of the Iraqi schools, were readily accessible only in Spain. Even there, following the fifteenth century expulsion of Arabs and Jews, Arabic was to become a little-known tongue and Saadia's works seemed permanently lost. It is a matter of record, however, that Saadia's thesis on the complementary relation between revelation and reason — adopted by Maimonides, who made it the foundation of a philosophical system — gained wide currency. Infused into the theology of Thomas Aquinas, foremost medieval Catholic thinker, it reached a Christian audience.

Nor is it any longer a news item that the entry of Arab invaders brought relief to the Jewish community of Spain. The free cross-fertilization of Hebrew and Arab cultures produced a renaissance in literature and philosophy, in science and religion. Even architecture boomed, as some of Spain's most celebrated churches confirm. They speak to the modern traveler of their glory long ago when they served a proud and wealthy Iberian Jewry as synagogues.

The long succession of distinguished Jews in Arab Spain began with Hasdai ibn-Shaprut (915–970), who held the most honorable post at the court of Abd-al-Rahman III. Another versatile Jew, Samuel ibn-Nagdela (d. 1055), rose to the highest position in Granada, one of the few Spanish provinces retaining its prestige during the Islamic regime. Like ibn-Shaprut, he was a gifted statesman, a discerning critic and writer, and a generous patron of learning. Unlike him, however, ibn-Nagdela rose from the humblest background.

In the literary domain also, Jews excelled under Spanish Arab rule. For despite powerful Iberian impulses, this was an extension of Middle East culture and political theory. The two most illustrious poets in medieval Jewish literature were Solomon ibn-Gabirol (c. 1021–c. 1058) and Judah Halevi (c. 1085–c. 1140). Both flourished in the Hispanic-Moslem environment of the eleventh-twelfth century. Heinrich Heine (1797–1856), a sensitive critic, called ibn-Gabirol "a nightingale singing in the darkness of the Gothic medieval world." Others, impressed with the texture of his verse and breadth of vision, ranked him with Dante and Milton. Toward life's sunset, ibn-Gabirol capped his reputation as a philosopher by writing *Fons Vitae* ("The Fountain of Life"). A little volume, it developed more fully his conception of God and the universe. Hailed by others still as a Jewish Plato, his most famous hymn, "The Royal Crown," is a series of beautiful poems extolling the magnificence of the Eternal.

Judah Halevi, an even more colorful personality, was "a wondrous, fiery pillar of song, guiding the mournful caravan of Israel through the wilderness of exile." His noblest genius found perfect expression in deathless love for Zion. All Jewish poets wrote more or less eloquently of Zion and wept for her widowhood, but to Halevi Zion was a genuine passion.

Hosts of other notable scholars, administrators, philosophers, and men of letters helped to create this golden age of Judaism.

By far the most impressive figure was Moses Maimonides (1135–1204) who best represented and summed up an era at the end of which he stood. "From Moses [the Lawgiver] to Moses [Mendelssohn], there arose none like unto Moses [Maimonides]," was the verdict of posterity upon him. As an expounder of Judaism, philosopher, and lover of learning, as a gentle, human character, few in Jewish history have surpassed him. A fervently pious Jew, he was nonetheless a man of tolerance who would not attack except when falsehoods were uttered. A Cordovan by birth, he was buried at Tiberias. He served the Cairo court of Saladin. There he was held in such high esteem that he declined an invitation to a similar post at the English court of Richard the Lion Heart. A Middle Eastern Arab by breeding, culture, and reputation, he was known as ibn-Maimun. All his books save one were composed in Arabic although written in Hebrew characters.

Contemplation of Jewish history in the broad outline of detail and episode seems to bear out the assumption that in the light of his record the Jew made a more substantially significant contribution as a child of the same Middle East that first reared him. Within that cultural-geographic framework of value and service, may be viewed, obvious exceptions notwithstanding, some of the major and most spectacular features of Judaism in the last two millenniums and before.

MIDDLE EAST TRIANGLE

In a drama, *Nathan the Wise*, Gotthold Ephraim Lessing (1729–1781) sets his scene in Jerusalem at the time of the Crusades. More important than the plot is the character of the trader, Nathan, a Jew who had come to look upon all religions as forms of one great truth. A Christian knight woos Nathan's adopted daughter, Recha. When the matter is brought to the attention of the Arab sultan, Saladin, all three faiths come into the closest of contact. Nathan's philosophy of religion is aptly illustrated by a story. A father possessed one valuable ring and three sons. He ordered two other rings made exactly like the original so that each son should receive a similar inheritance.

Lessing's philosophy of religion leaves much to be desired. It nevertheless reflects a historic Middle East situation with that basically unchanged triangle of Jewish-Christian-Moslem tension. The problem today is not so much that each of the three theistic faiths lays claim to an absolute finality. Nor is it that separation of Church and State has not yet established full freedom of conscience. The real issue today is that devotees of these great religions are not currently exerting enough positive influence upon society in behalf of peace and good will. In most instances, religious enthusiasm has been pressed into the service of divisive ends, and the result has been " the tinderbox of the Middle East."

Thus Judaism, to all intents and purposes, has surrendered to an emotional commitment to political, mundane ends. Christianity seems to be strikingly polarized. On the one hand, an Eastern, indigenous type is paralyzed by inferiority complexes and the fear of being swamped in an Islamic sea. On the other, a Western type is arrested by progressive policies at home and an inertia of silence abroad. Nor could the case be much different with an Islam, now portrayed, as in recent Egypt, by a Moslem brotherhood embodying an alliance between theological reaction and lust for political power; and now, as in Iran, throwing up a clerical agitator, a crossbreed, half saint and half demagogue. Apparently Islam has forsworn its vitality to reduce fear and to nerve people with confidence in divine mercy. In short, the defeatism of Middle East religion verifies the old Biblical truth enshrined in the story of Lot, nephew of Abraham. Lot's wife, it will be recalled, looked back and was instantly turned into a pillar of salt (Gen. 19:26).

One conclusion seems inescapable. Reaction, frustration, and social apathy are the lot of those who degrade religion by casting it in the role of fickle and immoral politics. Conversely, peace, good will, and reconstruction are the portion of those who seek the power of religion to change character by the conquest of fear, hatred, bitterness, and arrogance. It is then that an individual and collective consciousness becomes sensitive to the grace that shatters darkness and mitigates the perils of unforgiving hearts.

Thus to perpetuate the true record of Judaism at its noblest level is to safeguard all that that religion of a truly great though small people was intended to be. It is to seek, furthermore, an effective form of social, political, and economic responsibility. In a region aching for that full measure of freedom, neither militant Zionism nor its foster parent, anti-Semitism, has any place.

Jews, more particularly Israelis, willing to endorse the above concept might come along one step farther in their desire for peace with the Arabs and take two fundamental propositions into account. First, that no approach to the Middle East can carry permanent validity unless it takes seriously the history of the region, its internal structure, and the inner causes of its convulsions. Secondly, that the Middle East really becomes a problem when it encounters forces and impacts intent upon coercion and subjugation.

From hoary antiquity down to these latter days, the Middle East has not lacked for seers, prophets, apostles, and reformers. In our own time, back of each drive toward reform were the twin phenomena of craving for independence and passion for freedom. A Jewish record that neither vindicated the ancient Hebrew genius for law and justice nor fitted into the contemporary Middle East pattern might indeed run into foul weather as far into the future as any good and faithful friend of Judaism could predict.

If there is any single order of life in the region, it can be none other than Islam, the primary integrating principle of the Middle East. One of the most dismal developments of the twentieth century centers in the melancholy spectacle of a time-honored Judaism maneuvered into opposition to Islam by a militant Zionism. Thus Jew was pitted against Moslem while Christians ranged themselves on either side of the fence or took the even more shabby attitude of passive onlookers reveling in a neutral noncommitment.

The tie-up between militant Zionism and the Great Powers who supported the establishment of the State of Israel is a factor that militates against a peace settlement. Since Alexander and Caesar, imperialism elicits dread in the national consciousness. There is a point about the mouth of Dog River in the environs of Beirut dubbed an " open air museum " by the late Professor James Henry Breasted of Chicago. There one can read the inscriptions left by conquerors from Nebuchadnezzar and Rameses II to Napoleon III and the Twenty-first British Army Corps.

In order to justify itself imperialism employed every conceivable device and tactic. It adopted the policy of divide and rule and used exalted, humanitarian language, the lofty phraseology of religion and civilization. At the turn of the nineteenth century, the imperialists' stock in trade was the " Sick Man of Europe." The expression referred to an Ottoman ruler, both irresolute and corrupt, whose subjects stood in utter need of liberation and whose territories desperately awaited the colonizer's open season. In the Arab view, the State of Israel is the last episode in the chain of Western intrusive acts. Of course no one in his right mind will ever say that Judaism as such is a stranger to Middle East soil. As already stressed, the epochal phases of Jewish history are intimately associated with Palestine.

Yet the argument for the alien, imperialist, and intrusive character of Israel is based on these serious considerations. First, that Israel came into being through the declared will and initiative of foreign powers. Secondly, that the majority of leaders performing a responsible role in the State of Israel do not belong to Eastern Jewry. Thirdly, that the spirit and manner wherewith the Zionists chose to execute their plans were those of aggressive penetration and military conquest. Fourthly, that a militant, expansionist policy has seemed to inspire an evidently insatiable Zionism in the State of Israel.

Fifthly, that the intrusive and imperialist character of Israel is affirmed in the tragedy of the Arab refugees.

BASIS FOR DURABLE PEACE

There is hardly any need to reproduce further the nature of the conflict that rises before us. What we have here is the human tragedy in miniature form, with all the attributes of a demonic, disintegrating process. A hostility and an ill-will at present poison the Middle East, casting ominous shadows across the horizon. The late president Stephen B. L. Penrose of the American University of Beirut accurately reported in an article, " The Arabs Love Us No More," the heavy reverses sustained by America largely through its Palestine strategy.

There was not much evidence of a dove to relieve the monotony of border disputes and incidents. Nor did an olive branch offset the reciprocal exchange of acrimony. Nothing cheered those who longed for peace. At any rate, a marriage of convenience even if freely contracted would scarcely provide a sound foundation for future co-operation.

Only vision was left. The one hope to cherish and promote was that of a spiritual awakening. A meeting of minds between a few Jews, Christians, and Moslems who still believed in the efficiency of good will and trusted the power of sheer goodness might rule out conflict. Set in operation, the real constructive principle of the universe, namely, friendship, not fear, and love, not hatred, would win at last.

Any such change of heart would have started in the realm of humility and led to the confession that all we like sheep have gone astray. It would have rested in the prayer that only an Eternal helps formulate. It is thus that men cast aside the dead past and in forgiveness overcome the futilities of war and diplomacy. So to proceed would mean to retrieve the greatest power on earth in the light of a togetherness to serve both the Middle East and the whole world.

In *The Impact of Science Upon Society*, Bertrand Russell argued:

"We must learn not to say, 'Never! Better death than dishonor! . . .' Jews and Arabs will have to agree to submit to arbitration; if the award goes against the Jews, the President of the United States will have to insure the victory of the party to which he is opposed, since, if he supports the international authority, he will lose the Jewish vote in New York State. On the other hand, if the award goes in favor of the Jews, the Mohammedan world will be indignant, and will be supported by all the malcontents." (Pp. 75 f., 92, Simon and Schuster, Inc.)

Farther down in the book, Lord Russell arrives at a totally unexpected conclusion. "The root of the matter," he writes, "is a very simple and old-fashioned thing, a thing so simple that I am almost ashamed to mention it for fear of the derisive smile with which wise cynics will greet my words. The thing I mean — please forgive me for mentioning it — is love, Christian love or compassion. If you feel this, you have a motive for existence, a guide in action, a reason for courage, an imperative necessity for intellectual honesty."

In a word, Judaism has bequeathed to civilization a fabulous record which offers a clue to the lessening of tension in the region. To be secure where it is, Israel will need more than military strength. It will need to be true to its own history and increasingly to cultivate an indigenous consciousness alive to the nature and destiny of the Middle East. They only can become integral to that part of the world who know and serve those ultimates of truth and love and light in its tradition. "Not by might, nor by power, but by my Spirit, says the Lord of hosts" are the irrevocable words of Zechariah at a time of awakening and rebuilding in the ancient record of Judaism.

7

IMPACT OF PROTESTANT CHRISTIANITY

I T IS an inspiring fact that of the several titanic forces now swaying the Middle East, Christianity alone lays a just claim to historic antecedence and continuity in the region. Christianity stands alone as a great religion whose roots are deeper than those of Islam, nationalism, and Communism. It is of an earlier vintage than those types of Zionism, imperialism, and democracy currently invoked in the Middle East. None of Christianity's rivals, particularly Communism, can seriously match the spiritual resources of the Church.

The Middle East means something infinitely more than the historic battleground of Christianity and Islam. It is a veritable middle ground which since time immemorial has witnessed the interchange of arts and crafts, the mediation and assimilation of cultural and religious values. Cradle of three theistic faiths, it is probably the one sector of continental Asia where intercourse between the conflicting philosophies and religions of mankind yielded a degree of tangible universality.

The primary aim of this chapter is to discover and illustrate the nature of this intercourse in modern times, with special emphasis on the continuing impact of Christianity. It will not be easy, however, to reproduce even with a modicum of simplicity the bearing of Christianity on a region acknowledged as the focus of Western influence abroad. A difficulty stems directly from the fact that the Middle East occupies a favored position in the eyes of Westerners. They owe to it the beginnings of their cultural and religious heritage. How, it may well be asked, is one to speak of the Christian entry into a region which is itself the cradle of the Christian faith?

The answer is not far to seek. Much has happened in the domain of religious thought since the birth of Christ in Bethlehem of Judea. No greater responsibility devolves upon twentieth century Christianity than that of revival of the faith in and about the land where Jesus ministered.

The central thesis seems to be warranted, namely, that present-day Christianity, as heretofore, exerts a formidable influence on the Middle East. Preceding the birth of Mohammed, this influence was woven into the inner texture of the Koran. Through the living testimony of men and institutions, it contributed to the golden prime of the Caliphate. Research has abundantly shown that Christianity constituted a vital force in the lives of countless Moslem generations and in the total effort of Islamic peoples.

With the epic of Christian missions to the Middle East constantly before us, the treatment of the subject falls into four parts. First, an explication of the term "impact" and of the scope chosen for this inquiry. Secondly, an analysis of Islam in the light of its own ontology and the American Protestant thrust. Thirdly, an appraisal of this impact. Fourthly, the present-day and future outlook of Christianity's role in the region.

The Impact

"Impact" may be broadly defined as that impulse imparted by one who enjoys freedom in the truth to others whose spirituality is either dormant or morbid. To raise this issue is to ask whether anything distinctive and pulsating about the Christian religion really exists and may be communicated.

It ought to be observed at the outset that the whole idea of a Christian witness among non-Christians is an absurdity if it were to be construed primarily as the impress and shock of Christian culture. There can be no Christian strategy except where the truth shines through the human instrumentality to disturb the religious consciousness and shake the unbeliever from the stupor of unbelief.

Where the word "impact" might convey the notion of violence and collision, its Christian connotation is at once original and arresting. In this category, it refers to the givenness of grace as it fills the frail constitution of man, whose status as a prisoner to doubt makes him a creature deluded by selfish ends and cross-purposes.

The underlying dynamic is, therefore, of divine essence. Yet always assured the seeker is a freedom of choice, his privilege to accept or reject the overtures of the Eternal. In other words, the Christian impact upon individual lives is not realized through the enlistment of mercenary souls. Rather it is a voluntary acquiescence of mind, conscience, and heart in the thrust of Love incarnate.

This extraordinary influence is desperately needed by a generation, the world over, that has flagrantly tossed aside its patrimony of faith. It means the meeting of East and West, the abandonment of empty shibboleths and fetishes, the conquest of hate, fear, and defeatism. Above all, the fundamental unity of humanity is affirmed. Viewed in this perspective, the Middle East is ripe for the harvest. In its geographic and demographic configuration, it has been selected as one of the best laboratory cases in history for a study of the love of Christians for the non-Christian peoples.

Christianity's first modern surge in the region centered in Syria-Lebanon-Egypt and emanated from the strongholds of Eastern Orthodoxy, Roman Catholicism, and Protestantism, that is, from czarist Russia, Europe, and America. That the chief concern of this chapter is restricted to the impact of American Protestantism is partly due to the limitation of space. The fact remains, moreover, that American Protestantism acting through the ecumenical movement and the World Council of Churches exercises at present a conspicuous leadership and responsibility throughout Christendom.

Lebanon looms as an admirable seat of demonstration. Across the centuries, its Christian stock has had communion with both the Moslem East and the Christian West. From the beginning, Lebanon received the benefit of the impact. Within its confines, the missionary enterprise, launched in the nineteenth century, perhaps more than elsewhere attained a heartening fulfillment of its goals. Somewhat different causes combined to open up Iran and Egypt, but the priority of Lebanon will not be widely disputed.

Among the several denominations that occupied the field, New England Congregationalism and the Presbyterian Church, U.S.A., offer examples of uninterrupted contact with the indigenous peoples. Out of this came a far-reaching leavening which cannot be attributed to social, cultural, or any other humanistic origin. Discernible throughout was an underlying spiritual design, an expression of the phenomenon under discussion.

The argument persists, however, that the advent of American Protestantism forms a phase of Western cultural penetration. Yet if the genius of the impact as defined is borne in mind, this argument must certainly prove tenuous. Culture itself is not determined by race but is occasionally conditioned by a new environment. Likewise the challenge of Christianity in a given area is not fully explained by saying that it is a product of social, political, and economic dynamism.

That culture is not identical with race, society, or common tradition is an often forgotten reality. Anthropologically speaking, culture is a way of life adapted to a particular environment and involving a certain degree of social specialization, the channeling of energies along particular lines. The Eskimos of the Arctic and the Bushmen of South Africa exhibit cultures that are almost inseparable from race. But it is equally obvious that a few English and Irish emigrants, transplanted to Australia, in a hundred years produced a new human type, different culturally and psychologically from the parent society.

A new religious view of life can outweigh environment as a

factor that determines the nature of culture. Indeed, Islam as such, in its immediate aspects, offers a classic illustration of the kind of impact whereby the social mode of life was transmuted by a new religious enthusiasm. The Islamic ferment in the Middle East and certain parts of Europe, East Asia, and Central Africa gave rise to social institutions which modified the status quo. It blurred the divisive character of race, geography, and former political allegiance. Of necessity, therefore, before the ferment of Christianity in the Middle East is appraised, Islam must be considered.

ISLAM AND THE PROTESTANT THRUST

An exposition of historic Islam may help to reveal the core of Middle East culture and the nature of the American Protestant thrust.

1. *Ontology of Islam.* When Abraham Kuyper (1837–1920), the Dutch theologian and statesman, returned from a visit to the eastern shores of the Mediterranean, he began to compose his three-volume *Pro Rege,* an interpretation of Christ's Kingship in every domain of existence. In the Moslem world, Kuyper had discovered that the name of Mohammed stood highest in the affections of the masses. The faithful Moslem paid homage to Mohammed about four to five times during each of the 1,800 to 2,500 prayers which he annually offered. The ontology of the Moslem, that is, his outlook on being and reality, is built around this profound reverence for the Prophet.

How did this come to pass? The medieval Arab drama opened with a series of rapid forays which swept the followers of Mohammed into Syria and Iraq, Egypt and Iran. Then they turned westward into North Africa and the Iberian Peninsula, and eastward into India and lands beyond. Powerful folkways, from Arabia as well as the conquered lands, swallowed the native cultures much as the footprints of an elephant swallow up those of other creatures. The Middle East became the home base of a cosmopolitan civilization amidst whose arts, crafts, science, philosophy, literature, and religion stood the figure of Mohammed.

This Islamic system survived the Mongol invasion of Baghdad (1258), and, until World War I, its chief militant defenders were the Ottoman Turks. A repercussion from Judaeo-Christianity, Islam had its own characteristics. Chief among these were the personality of the founder, and the unique role of Arabic speech. Characteristic, too, were a Koranic theory of revelation, an institution of brotherhood which united the believers in a closed circle, and an extreme structural simplicity. There was no great emphasis on God's redemptive purpose.

The aesthetic and spiritual aspects of Islam were made more deserving of Christian compassion by the grave stagnation which overtook the Moslem peoples during the period of Western upheaval. Al-Ghazzali, Avicenna, and Averroës had excelled their peers of the Latin West and rendered decisive contributions to the Christian philosophy of the age. Sixteenth century Islam, however, saw no rehabilitation of theology, experienced no religious revival, knew no Reformation or Renaissance, and produced hardly anyone equal to Martin Luther, Erasmus, or John Calvin.

The grim and melancholy character of Islamic theology unfortunately was aggravated during the seventeenth and eighteenth centuries. It left no doubt that this system was impotent by the sheer force of its own resources to stem the tide of decadence in the Middle East. There was an absence of visible, aesthetic representation. Painting, sculpture, and drama did not exist. The primary achievement of the Islamic Middle East had been verbalizing. Its nonverbal contributions were in the fields of architecture, miniature painting, and decorative art. The single keynote of Islamic culture seems to have been simplicity of organization. On the pietistic level, there was an ostensible surrender to the will of Allah, without much concern, however, for the cathartic purposes of the Creator. There was no real commitment to his love, no unselfish regard for the welfare of non-Moslems. Providence had been reduced to Fate, and the fear of Fate, which in the language of Kierkegaard is the fear of nothing, tended to vitiate the norms of ethics and public morality.

2. *The American Protestant Thrust.* Words fail to describe
the enormity of the task that faced the American educator in
the nineteenth century Middle East. Here was an Islamic culture as cut off from its ancient moorings as it was alien to the
mainsprings of the modern world. The maximum duration of
Islamic culture was seven centuries, A.D. 571 to A.D. 1258. Military ascendancy was practically over by A.D. 1050, as the success of the First Crusade a half century later suggests. There
have been no re-creations or renascences since. The Persian
and Turkish movements relied heavily on ethnic revival and
are recognized by some authorities as conscious secessions
from the more genuinely Arab-Islamic tradition.

What were the assets that the American Protestant brought
to the alleviation of physical and religious distress in a society
that had struck its lowest ebb? Professor Kenneth Scott Latourette ably demonstrated the magnificent job that the American Churches performed at home when they followed and
nurtured the population in its march toward ever-receding
frontiers. The Churches held the immigrants from Europe to
their faith. Christian agencies reached out to the non-Christian
elements in the country, notably the Jews and Orientals.

Looking to more distant horizons, the Churches evinced concern for lands beyond the seas. Classical American culture
bore the imprint of this Protestant dynamism, which about
1820 was ready to leap into the Middle East. Foreshadowed by
representatives of the Church Missionary Society, and others,
the first two short-lived pioneers of the American Board were
Pliny Fisk (1792–1825) and Levi Parsons (1792–1822). They
landed at Malta on December 23, 1819, and later proceeded to
Smyrna, Beirut, and Jerusalem.

Only a few decades after the Republic was established, this
American Protestant thrust began. In the formative period
(1820–1914) teachers from the New World had instilled in
their pupils something of the political philosophy that had inspired the American Revolution. The discrepancies between
the concept of freedom in the truth of God and in the deistic

credo of some front-line figures among the founding fathers were obvious. Yet the early missionaries almost intuitively communicated the ideals of statesmen such as Washington, Jefferson, Franklin, and Hamilton.

The primary aim, however, was religious and educational, having no official connection with the American government. Through church, school, hospital, printing press, and by dint of personal example, the bigotry and ignorance of a static society were slowly overcome. The Arabic translation of the Bible was initiated in 1849 by Eli Smith (1802–1857) and brought to completion in 1864 (with the collaboration of Lebanese scholars) by Cornelius V. A. Van Dyck (1818–1895). It remains a testimony to the work of pioneers and a torch in erudition. George Antonius, famed chronicler of the Arab awakening, was eminently right when he ascribed the modern Arab revival more to the influence of American education than to any other single factor. No foreign-born educator has yet succeeded as Presbyterian Cornelius V. A. Van Dyck did in identifying himself with the Middle East. For his Christian piety, learning, and espousal of their common cause, the Arabs regard him as one of their own foremost luminaries.

AN APPRAISAL OF THE IMPACT

It was partly due, then, to the influence of Christianity in its Protestant form that the Middle East saw the dawn of a new era. Stirred up and shaken into the vigor of throbbing life, the total existence of a people seemed to hang in the balance. Whereas a complete rupture with medievalism and reaction was slow in coming, the Islamic mentality tended to abandon archaic institutions in favor of a forward look. And although, as already noted, the Protestant impact must not be confused with culture, nothing could prevent its reverberations from reaching nationalist and secular circles. Thence it re-echoed in the political and social domains of the vast Moslem world.

Writing in 1900, Dr. Henry H. Jessup of the Syria Mission recalled the words of the 1849 report of the standing committee on the translation of the Bible into Arabic. A prophetic passage in that report had said:

" The Arab translator is interpreting the lively oracles for the forty millions of an undying race whose successive and ever augmenting generations shall fail only with the final termination of all earthly things. Can we exaggerate on such a theme? Is it easy to overestimate the importance of that mighty power that shall send the healing leaves of salvation down the Tigris, the Euphrates, the Nile, and the Niger; that shall open the living fountains in the plains of Syria, the deserts of Arabia, and the sands of Africa; that shall gild with the light of life the craggy summits of goodly Lebanon and sacred Sinai and giant Atlas? " (*Brief Documentary History of the Translation of the Scriptures Into the Arabic Language,* Preface, American Press, Beirut.)

Nearly six decades have now passed since Jessup embodied these words in the documentary history of the Arabic translation of the Scriptures. Is it possible today more fully to see the outcome of missions in the Middle East? A balance sheet of the region's recent transformation will show a number of achievements distinctly traceable to Protestant initiative. These may be said to constitute the concrete evidence of the impact and to provide the groundwork for further investigation.

Looking upon these achievements, one may resort to a descriptive metaphor and suggest that the impact possessed a prismatic character. Rather than limit itself to its own peculiar heritage, American education was noteworthy for the refraction of light drawn from diverse sources. It developed an interpretative genius, breaking the light down into its component parts, albeit within the framework of a Christian spectrum. For its integrating and informing principle, it relied upon the doctrine that upheld the unity of mankind. It is to the eternal credit of the Protestant educator in this strategic region that he taught the concept of unity in diversity. His work manifests itself along six levels which are by no means mutually exclusive.

1. The level of Arab nationalism, where the idea of autonomy was fostered. This is not the place to expound the origin

of the Arab League and its ups and downs, or to trace the beginning of the Arab states. It is undoubtedly true, however, that Protestant education was more responsible than any other agency of its kind for training the men who administered public and private affairs. In a sense, it prepared the way for independence. Under Lord Cromer and throughout Great Britain's occupation of Egypt (1882–1922), valiant service to the cause of good government and efficient administration was rendered by graduates of the Syrian Protestant College.

2. Islamic rehabilitation and the rediscovery of the wellsprings of Moslem religious thought along lines that were compatible with free inquiry and the demands of a new age. Whether in Egypt, Syria, or Pakistan, the leaders who pioneered in intellectual, religious, and social reconstruction were men who had listened long and attentively to the Protestant voice. Eminent Moslems such as the Indian Ahmad Khan (1817–1888), Ameer Ali (1849–1928), Mohammed Iqbal (1876–1938); the Egyptian Mohammed Abduh (1849–1905) and Qasim Amin (1865–1908) — male champion of woman's rights; as well as later Syrian Moslem thinkers such as Abd-al-Qadir al-Maghribi and Mohammed Kurd Ali, were sufficiently fascinated by Protestant thought to know what Islam must do to survive.

3. The revival of indigenous Christianity. This came about through the resuscitation of Eastern communions and the replacement of their air of frustration and withdrawal with an awakened concern for the uplift of the Middle East. The Coptic Church of Egypt, the Eastern Orthodox patriarchates, the Maronite Church, the Armenian Gregorian Church, and other venerable offshoots experienced a new surge of life. Despite centuries of virtual confinement, these Churches had remained at least nominally consistent in their allegiance to the faith. Now they began to close their ranks and restate their religion in terms of witness and service.

4. The level of integrating the several competing impacts — British, French, Muscovite, Roman Catholic, and other — in an

abiding unity of thought and purpose. Though primarily American in inception, the Protestant influence did not seek either to promote a peculiarly American political system or to reproduce itself in an American cultural progeny. Lebanon became a Middle East Switzerland, not only as a summer resort but, in a deeper sense, as a land where a true democratic outlook tolerated the coexistence of seemingly irreconcilable groups and philosophies.

5. The integration of the cultural, religious, economic, and political phases of existence in a harmony calculated to halt the further deterioration of the Middle East. Less an expression of pragmatic philosophy, this was a corollary of the Reformed Calvinistic concern for the secular order. It engendered a consciousness sensitive to the individual's duties toward the Church, community, and state.

6. The establishment of a national evangelical Church which in a city such as Beirut fulfilled a priestly function in the service of the community. Physical evidence of success in this direction is demonstrable in the rise of ecclesiastical bodies among which the ranking assemblies are the Synod of Syria-Lebanon and the Synod of the Nile. The four stages in the development of Protestant missions — from pioneer work to the formation of a mission Church, and from independent Church to partnership between national and missionary forces — were thus spanned. This is a tangible result of lasting significance.

OUTLOOK

Viewed in this light, the responsibility of Christianity in the Middle East takes on new meaning with each succeeding generation. This meaning is discovered as we peer into the future in terms of ecumenicity and sound learning. Taking stock of the crucial issues that agitate contemporary man, ecumenicity will avoid divided counsels in the household of faith and will exert a concerted effort in order to translate love into a living reality.

In the mid-twentieth century, an auspicious record of more than a hundred years of devoted service stood in jeopardy. Admitting their heavy indebtedness to Woodrow Wilson, as author of the doctrine of self-determination of peoples, the Moslems of the Middle East averred that he was the selfsame American President who allowed the Balfour Declaration to be issued. The victory of militant Zionism in Great Britain, America, and the Middle East, although not necessarily foreseen by Mr. Wilson, was thus assured. Despite the long period of American indifference (1922–1933), the triumph of Zionism, furthered by the Nazi atrocities, was a foregone conclusion.

Informed Moslem leaders contended, furthermore, that American policy did not cease to favor the State of Israel at the expense of the Islamic peoples. From all this, the Moslem drew the inescapable conclusion that the Western democracies were intent upon his destruction. Sensitive to this frenzied state of mind, the Christian tried to understand one to whom he went out as a friend. But the Christian of necessity saw the tragic Islamic figure against the background of more gruesome forces which menaced the modern world.

These forces gravitated toward two different though not altogether unrelated points: (1) the international political setting where Communism and the need to rid the world of its evils represented the crisis of our time; (2) the sphere of religion where the outlook was darkened by uncertainty in so many minds with regard to the essence of faith and the mandate of Christianity to call men to a regenerative way of life.

1. That Christianity stood athwart the advance of Communism in the Middle East requires but little elucidation. In its distinctive way, Christianity offered the elements of a lasting solution to the millions who in utter despair turned to Karl Marx and the pseudo religion devised by his heirs and interpreters. How did the assets of Christianity stack up in this embattled sphere?

When the ancient city of Athens was stricken with famine, its delegates stood before the elders of Sparta and, pointing to their empty bags, cried, " These bags are empty, fill them." To which the laconic Spartans replied, "We know that empty bags must be filled." The modern Communists, with ostensible solicitude for the welfare of the depressed masses, served their own ends even as they phrased their propaganda in language reminiscent of the often unpracticed ethics of Christianity.

But the empty bags of the Middle East, and of all the world's underprivileged, were not actually filled by the subtle jargon of a dictatorship that had surpassed czarist Russia in lust for power and imperial domination. Only those who were constrained by a consuming love for their brother man could objectively serve the downtrodden of the earth. It was therefore clear that neither Communism nor a Christianity which had lost its essential character could touch the heart of the Middle East. Were the mighty battalions of the Soviet Union completely crushed on the field of battle, the real defeat of Communism would not yet have been achieved. The evil which was Communism was only to be overcome when men were won to the kind of faith that translated itself into service, partnership in knowledge, and the sharing of all good things.

The heart of the matter is that nations, even more than the individuals who compose them, are quarrelsome, suspicious, and jealous of each other. Only men imbued with the spirit of compassion can begin to obliterate ignorance, heal body and soul, and impart technology. Otherwise what happened in China could repeat itself in the Middle East. The Chinese students, say of a Christian university such as Yenching in Peking, provided some of the best cadres of the Chinese Communist Army. The question for the Church, the key to its victory over Communism in the Middle East and elsewhere, consisted less in its capability to feed the people and more in whether or not it was inspired by One who fed the multitudes by the sea.

2. As regards the purely religious sphere, the problem involved nothing less than a rigorous heart-searching by Christians concerned with the basic affirmations of their faith. To

win through in the Middle East, Christians had to know what and whom they believed. Only then did they bestir themselves to new endeavors. In this respect they did emulate the example of nineteenth century pioneers, but in no case did they rest upon the laurels of those saints of a former generation whose testimony was truly great.

James F. Riggs, in an article which appeared in the first volume of the *Princeton Theological Review* (1903) on the subject, " Missionary Policy in the Levant," recommended "a resolute concentration of our available energies in two lines, namely, (1) education, and (2) publication." In the immediate future, these two channels of grace will continue to promote the impact of Christianity upon the Middle East, although with a renewed sense of direction and greater precision of objectives.

Whereas it is impossible to give a precise formula covering all that Christian education ought to be, in the Middle East its three stages seem to be didactic, methodical, and substantial. The didactic stage means the free impartation of knowledge, ranging from the campaign against illiteracy to Western learning and the wisdom of the ages, wherein the heritage of the Middle East itself ranks high. The methodical stage involves among other phases the inculcation of proficiency in the arts and sciences, technology, as well as the professional skills and intellectual disciplines. The substantial stage basically is the interpretation of religion as a way of life. When this last stage shall have received the serious attention of dedicated men, no one will need any longer to feel apprehensive for the future impact of Christianity upon the Middle East. Given an effective solidarity between national and missionary personnel; given a Middle East ecumenicity that shall rise in strength, bearing the marks of piety and sound learning; and, above all, given a new generation of Christians with a profound comprehension of what Christianity really signifies, the future impact of Christianity upon the Middle East may well surpass the past.

8

AN ISLAMIC CULTURAL PATTERN

THERE can scarcely be real understanding, let alone evaluation, of the Middle East apart from a critical account of its Islamic cultural pattern. Embodied in a historical medieval experience, this pattern is nowhere completely forgotten. It is eminently alive and dynamic in shaping the contemporary mentality of the region's peoples as well as in directing the course of their international relations. Exercising a certain degree of selectivity, we may assume that at its best the Islamic pattern disclosed itself in science, philosophy, and literature.

It is not proposed, however, to introduce at this juncture a historical sketch of medieval Arab science, philosophy, and literature. Especially where scholarly opinion is divided, moreover, it would be nothing short of folly to cover up controversial issues by offering a hurried summary. Yet it might not be out of order to ask the one question ordinarily missed: What is the meaning for today's Middle East of the region's fabulous heritage of technical and intellectual achievement originating in medieval times?

Such a direct confrontation with the fundamental issue of meaning will naturally disregard a great deal that is quite obviously irrelevant. The things that concern us most here are the very quality of mind and attributes of the spirit bequeathed by medieval Islamic civilization. It is not for us to whitewash or condemn, but rather to ponder and weigh its content in order to depict what is meaningful to this generation.

SCIENCE

A number of the presuppositions of Islamic science are revealing. They include the idea that science transcends barriers of race and creed. Also, that an enlightened ruler ought to foster scientific activity; that a man of science is to be held in high honor; and that the unity of all knowledge must be affirmed. Similarly held was the view that cultures are interdependent, that research must push back the frontiers of knowledge. Above all, it was maintained that there are limits to reason and bounds beyond which finite truth cannot go. These postulates can be substantiated from the annals of Arab medieval science.

Not all Arab by birth or Moslem by persuasion, the majority of the scientists concerned were nonetheless Islamic in so far as they lived and labored in the shadow of the faith, and Arab since they used Arabic in the transmission of their ideas. In A.D. 1268, Bar Hebraeus — primate of the Syrian Jacobite Church — arrived at the intellectual center of Maraghah in Persia to deliver a set of lectures on Euclid. Several years later this illustrious historian of science, celebrated as the last classical author in Syriac literature, reappeared at the same seat of learning in order to teach Ptolemy in Arabic. In this personage and event there is a symbol of the universal aspect of Arab science, transcending social, historical, and geographic barriers.

The first bona fide institute of advanced study in the Arab world was the Baghdad House of Wisdom initiated by the caliph al-Mamun in A.D. 830. In addition to its translation bureau, this institute became the envy of scholarship by reason of its academy, public library, and the observatory attached to it. Here the caliph's astronomers not only made systematic observations of the celestial bodies but also verified with remarkable accuracy all the fundamental elements of Ptolemy's almagest: the obliquity of the ecliptic, the procession of the equinoxes, and the length of the solar year. To this observatory al-Mamun soon added another on Mt. Qasiyun, outside of Damascus. The equipment in those days consisted of quadrant, astrolabe, dial, and globes.

In his comment on the high esteem in which the enlightened al-Mamun regarded scientists, Bar Hebraeus wrote: "He was not ignorant that they are the elect of God, his noblest and most useful servants, whose lives are devoted to the improvement of their rational faculties. . . . The teachers of wisdom are the true luminaries and legislators of the world, which but for their aid would once more sink into ignorance and barbarism." (*Arab Heritage,* ed. by N. A. Faris, pp. 247 f., Princeton University Press.)

Al-Mamun's fine example was emulated by succeeding princes of the house of Abbas, their rivals the Fatimids of North Africa, the Umayyads of Spain, and others. The same royal concern with science and the scientists was espoused by the independent emirs of distant provinces. This emulation diffused the taste for and reward of science from Samarqand and Bukhara to Fez and Cordova.

Arab science throve between the times, between Greek decay and the Renaissance. Its importance consists not so much in its originality as in the fact that in the long interval which separated the evanescence of Greek learning from the rebirth of Europe it preserved the unity of Western traditions. This unity of all science, wisdom, and knowledge is reflected in the very genesis of Arab technical thought. From it Europe derived not merely philosophical and scientific ideas but, more significantly, a secret of its dynamic energy and motivating power.

The rendition into Arabic of the Greek manuscripts, whether directly or through intermediary Syriac versions, was largely effected under the patronage of the early Abbasid caliphs at Baghdad (c. A.D. 750–850). The work was accomplished by skillful and painstaking scholars who were for the most part Syrians, Hebrews, or Persians, of the Christian, Jewish, Zoroastrian, or pagan faith. Thus devotion to the unity of knowledge and the interdependence of all culture took visible form. After a checkered career in the East, Arab science passed over to the Western Islamic community in Spain and thence made a deeper impression on Christian and Jewish thought than it had had on the Moslems themselves. Other scientists finally carried the torch into northeast Italy, where it prepared the way for the rebirth of the classics.

Yet the unity of science did not blind the Arab mind in matters of epistemology to the limits of reason and the insufficiency of finite truth. Greece introduced man's thought to the prospect of controlling nature, and lured him with the concept that science is the center of things, and the far more perverted notion that man is the measure of all things. It followed, with perfect logic, therefore, that the world had merely to be analyzed, organized, and dominated by man. This was the acme of Greek thought, and it was a far cry from the nobler teaching of Islam, which came infinitely closer to the implications of Biblical revelation. For the gods of the Greeks were the projections of great men, and not always good men.

When the total picture of Arab science is contemplated in retrospect, it seems to extend over almost five hundred years, from the eighth to the thirteenth century. During this time the frontiers of the unknown were constantly receding. Science and technology in this epoch may be reduced to five classes — mathematics, astronomy, physics, chemistry, and medicine. Advance in these fields may be tentatively highlighted in what follows.

In mathematics, the foundation was laid as far back as A.D. 772, when an unknown Indian astronomer introduced the Hindu numerals. These, in the subsequent century, were passed into the West by al-Khwarizmi. The latter's name is the source of the word "algorism," and his standard work included in its title the expression *al-jabr* (restoration), whence our "algebra." Among later mathematicians influenced by al-Khwarizmi were Omar Khayyám, Leonardo Fibonacci of Pisa (d. after 1240), and Master Jacob of Florence. The latter's Ital-

ian treatise on mathematics, dated A.D. 1307, comprises the six
types of quadratic equations cited by Moslem mathematicians.

No less striking was the transformation wrought in astrology
and its offspring astronomy. The pioneer astronomers made
their bow in the early ninth century, led by al-Farghani, Albu-
masar, and al-Kindi. Al-Battani (d. 929) made astronomical
observations at al-Raqqah in Iraq and Antioch, Syria. He cor-
rected some of Ptolemy's results previously taken on trust. He
compiled new tables showing by calculations the orbit of the
sun, moon, and certain planets.

Perhaps independently of an earlier Indian scholar, al-
Battani, whose Latin name was Albategnius, introduced the
use of the sine, in calculation, and particularly that of the tan-
gents. He proved the possibility of annual or sun eclipses and
accurately computed the obliquity of the ecliptic, the duration
of the tropical year and seasons, and the true mean orbit of
the sun. His best-known tables, preserved in manuscript form
at the Vatican Library, were published by Melanchthon, the
associate of Martin Luther, at Nuremberg in 1537.

Arab astronomy, transported to Spain, blossomed at Cordova and Toledo. From the latter city the Toledan Tables,
drawn by al-Zarqali in A.D. 1080, took their name, were rendered into Latin in the twelfth century by Gerard of Cremona,
and were similarly absorbed (c. 1140) into the system of Raymond of Marseilles. Al-Zarqali, foremost astronomer of the
time, was the first to prove the notion of the solar apogee with
reference to the stars. According to his instruments it amounted
to 12.04″, whereas its true value is 11.8″. In *De revolutionibus
orbium coelestium*, Copernicus quotes both al-Zarqali and al-
Battani.

The physics of Plato's Academy and Aristotle's Lyceum, as
it was not built on experimentation but argument, retarded the
progress of real scientific knowledge. It is to be deplored that
the metaphysics of the Infinite has often been enlisted in the
services of superstition. Yet, undeniably, the human faculties
were fortified by the art and practice of dialectics. The ten
predicaments of Aristotle collect and methodize our ideas, and

his syllogism is the keenest weapon of dispute. These, too, were dexterously wielded by the Arab thinkers.

The science of chemistry owes its inception to tireless Arab industry. The two principal operations of calcination and reduction were scientifically described. Improvement was made in the methods for evaporation, sublimation, melting, and crystallization. Arab chemists knew how to prepare crude sulphuric and nitric acids and to mix them in order to produce aqua regia, in which gold and silver could be dissolved. In general they modified the Aristotelian theory of the constituents of metals in a way that survived, with but slight alterations, until the beginning of modern chemistry in the eighteenth century.

They first invented and named the alembic for the purposes of distillation, analyzed the substances of the three kingdoms of nature, and converted the poisonous minerals into soft and salutory medicines.

In medicine, the names of Masawayh, Jabir, al-Razi, and Avicenna deserve to be classed with those of the Greek masters. The first, a Christian physician, failing to obtain human subjects for dissection (a practice discouraged by Islam), had recourse to apes. Arab interest in the healing science found support in the prophetic tradition: science is twofold, theology and medicine. A physician, combining the functions of philosopher, theologian, and healer, rated by virtue of his many-sided office as hakeem, that is, man of wisdom.

In the curative use of drugs some remarkable advances were made. Arab druggists established the first apothecary shops, founded the earliest school of pharmacy, and produced the first pharmacopoeia. Like physicians, they were required to submit to a test. In A.D. 931, Baghdad had over 880 physicians, licensed to exercise their lucrative profession. In Spain, the life of a Roman Catholic princess was once entrusted to the skill of Arab medical men, and the school of Salerno, their legitimate offspring, revived in Italy and Europe the forgotten precepts for the relief of suffering.

It is clear, then, that the Middle Ages were not quite so dark as certain medievalists once reported. From the second half of the eighth to the end of the eleventh century, Arabic was the scientific language of mankind. Anyone with ambition for culture had to study that language, just as today mastery of a Western language is a prerequisite to intellectual advancement. Yet all that is merely a record with little meaning apart from those immutable qualities of mind and spirit which made the medieval course of Islamic science possible and which possess a continuing validity for the present and future.

PHILOSOPHY

The most impressive body of speculative thought known to the medieval civilization of the Mediterranean world was that of Arab philosophy. It did not stem from pre-Islamic Arabian wisdom, but was Greek in origin, too. Mediated through Syriac Christian scholars, it fashioned a synthesis which took into account the claims of its own time and environment. From the period when the Arabs introduced Aristotle into Spain in the tenth century, he became for medieval thought and science what Newton is to the modern world. The readmission of Aristotle into the bloodstream of Western science and religion wrought a transformation in Christian philosophy and theology.

Arab philosophy was less a commentary on Aristotle, however, than an inquiry into the nature of ultimate reality. Avicenna, prince of Arab philosophers, strove, like Aristotle, to construct a metaphysics that made being as such its main concern. Culminating in Averroës, this philosophy established a theory of knowledge undergirding certitude regarding the eternity of God. It might be useful in what follows to examine this system of thought at closer range.

The most crucial event in European history since the Punic Wars was the triumph of Moslem arms in the eighth century, a hundred years after the death of Mohammed. Roman antiquity came to a halt, and while Europe was only beginning to be Byzantinized, the Middle Ages fell upon it. Almost simultaneously, a new Christian civilization — neither Greek nor Latin, but Nordic — was struggling to be born. A new Europe would emerge under Teutonic auspices and Christendom, though battered by its Moslem adversary, would reconstruct a new Roman Empire and regain the Greek heritage, aided by what Arab philosophers were able to transmit.

Yet the intellectual contribution which the Arab-Islamic civilization rendered to the new West did not exactly originate in the Arabian Peninsula. Surely the pre-Islamic Arabians boasted a repository of keen observations of nature centering in the life and fate of man. Within their peculiar categories, the Arabians achieved a reputation in the ancient Semitic world, as the Old Testament proves. The Koran (31:11, 12) reproduces the name of a sage Luqman, paragon of wisdom among the ancient Arabs. This oral tradition of wisdom is not, however, the subsoil of that later Arab philosophy which radiated from the centers of Islamic culture and exerted a decisive influence upon Europe.

The philosophy that Islamic writings enshrine is traceable to the Greek studies of Syrian Christian scholars. Having acquired classical philosophy and science from the Syrians, the thinkers of Islam fashioned these into a new synthesis observing the demands of their own era with its cosmopolitan society. For the origins of Arab philosophy, therefore, we must turn to the advanced civilization of the Middle East which became subject to Arab authority in the seventh century.

The Hellenization of western Asia had proceeded since the days of Alexander of Macedon (356–323 B.C.). Alexandria and Antioch attained fame as the centers of Greek culture. With the spread of Christianity, interest in the classical heritage deepened. In order to comprehend the New Testament, ecclesiastical canons and decrees, as well as the writings of the Church Fathers, the Christians of Syria had to learn the Greek language and literature.

But the seventh century Moslems were hardly ready for the implications of Greek logic and philosophy. However, their capacity for philosophical discipline and inquiry was sharpened as converts from Christianity and Judaism began to swell their ranks. By the eighth century, the first Islamic school of philosophy, that of the Qadarites, made its appearance in Syria partly as a reaction against Koranic determinism. Its major concern, the problem of free will, became a primary tenet of the rationalist Mutazilite school, which came to its own under the early rulers of the Abbasid caliphate (750–1258) of Baghdad. Dynamic Greco-Syrian ideas were already beginning to register in the theological controversies that stirred the Moslem world.

The orthodox Islamic reaction to the philosophical trend in theology was spearheaded in the tenth century by al-Ashari (873–935) of Baghdad. He evolved a new dialectic receptive to Greek reason but thoroughly grounded in Koranic thought. The Mutakallimun (dialecticians) were Islamic speculators who subordinated philosophy to revealed religious truth. A harmony of faith and reason, religion and philosophy, was meantime shaping up as the goal of philosophers. It was attempted by their ranking representatives, the Arab al-Kindi (d. c. 873), the Turk al-Farabi (c. 870–950), and the Persian ibn-Sina (Avicenna, 980–1037).

The achievements of these men who lived in the Middle East were climaxed in ibn-Rushd (Averroës, 1126–1198), who belonged to the annals of Spanish Islam. Yet the Moslem philosophers may be said to have passed through Islam without fully becoming integrated in its basic thought pattern. Although influenced by philosophy in his early career, al-Ghazzali (1058–1111) — Islam's foremost theologian — turned in his maturity to Sufi mysticism. In his major works he enunciated the fundamental affirmation that religious knowledge must inevitably depend upon revelation.

The orthodox Mutakallimun rose to the defense of the Islamic faith. Their apologetic seemed to center in the problem of creation. Against the Aristotelian idea that the universe is fixed and matter eternal, they advanced a theory of particles (atoms), based on Democritus. It upheld the view that the energy of God is in perpetual action, vitalizing the very particles of the created objects which, therefore, live and move and have their being by the constant flow of divine life. Thus bodies come into existence or die through the aggregation or sunderance of the particles. Not only space, but time also was allegedly made up of small individual moments. Once the creation of the world was established on these grounds, it was an easy matter for the apologists to confirm the existence of the Creator, the validity of prophecy, and the immortality of the soul.

That the science of Aristotle triumphed over the Democritean theory of particles, espoused by the Mutakallimun, and over the Platonist concepts current in the Moslem world, is not essential to the understanding of Arab philosophy in its world-wide relations. What is of the essence is that after the Arabs introduced Aristotle to Spain in the tenth century, he became for medieval science what Newton's physics is to the modern world.

Aristotelian science began from the thesis that the real world is the sensed one. Ideas and concepts which did not originate in sense perception did not constitute part of reality's core. By the chemical constituents of all things — earth, air, fire, and water — was meant the qualified bits of the total manifold of nature. Therefore to be is to possess sensed properties which are actualized in concrete nature as positive forms.

Thus, the soul of man was identified with the rational body. God was likewise identified with the cosmos as the Unmoved Mover, the Rational Principle, approximately but never completely actualized in matter. Once the logical character of Aristotle's forms was conceded, the eternity of God and the immortality of the soul followed in neat order.

Hence it is obvious that the transformation wrought by the readmission of Aristotle into the bloodstream of Western science and religion must be discovered not within the orbit of Islam but in Christian philosophy and theology. Until Arab thinkers rescued Aristotle from obscurity in the West, Augustinian theology had had for its philosophical framework a theory grounded in Plotinus and Plato. It held that the sensed world is not real and that the sensed self is but the symbol of the more ideal and immortal soul beyond. With the entry of Aristotle into the sphere of Christian theology, a new approach to ultimate reality was deemed necessary.

Arab speculation was steeped in practically the entire content of Greek thought. From the Sophists, it acquired logical analysis of what was involved in description and definition. From Socrates came a concern with the meaning of the " concept," raising it from the world of shadows to that of particulars. Aristotle offered an analysis of thing as well as of thought and was hailed in the medieval and Islamic world as the unrivaled First Teacher.

Aristotle emerged as the ideal champion of a movement that drew its authority from his works, whether they were authentically or apocryphally ascribed to him. From these works arose the problems that exercised medieval philosophy and endowed it with distinction. Yet the writings of Arab philosophers, the more carefully they are scrutinized, turn out to be less the works of exegesis and commentary than an expression of calm inquiry. This was the chief peculiarity of that intellectual development represented above all by Avicenna and Averroës.

In addition to his medical *Canon,* Avicenna's *Healing* contained the logic, metaphysics, physics, and philosophy by which his name became deservedly celebrated. Molded by Greek insights, this work had the merit of reconciling Aristotle and Plotinus in a simple, refreshing manner. The central theme, to which everything else seemed subsidiary, was that of being. There lay Aristotle's chief contribution to the making of medieval philosophy.

Avicenna interpreted being in the light of empirical psychology and relied on concepts drawn from the Neoplatonic theory of emanation. The hierarchy of being — vegetable, animal, and rational — was apexed by the First Principle, the sovereign and indivisible One who is God. From the First Principle emanated the First Intelligence. The world of ideas dawned as a series of pure intelligences which animated the celestial bodies. The highest body to be thus animated was the sphere of the fixed stars. From this emanated a soul which animated the planets of which the moon was considered the lowest. From the soul and body of the sphere-moon sprang the Active Intelligence which gave rise to the human soul and the four elements.

This world of being involving a series of intelligibles became part of the Western scholastic tradition. Trends in this direction appeared when Albertus Magnus (c. 1193–1280) and his contemporaries adopted the intelligibles of Avicenna and referred to them as intellects.

Averroës wrote *Incoherence of Incoherence,* a reply to the attack on rationalism which al-Ghazzali had embodied in his *Incoherence of the Philosophers.* He sought to reconcile Islamic dogma with the results of philosophy. In his defense of the eternity of the world — which precluded *creatio ex nihilo* — he incurred the enmity of Moslem theologians. The thirteenth century Church was also compelled to proscribe what it believed to be his doctrines. Though eternal, the world, according to Averroës, has a Prime Mover who himself is eternal and who is constantly endowing creation with dynamic. The two forms of eternity are, therefore, to be differentiated, since the one is with, the other without, cause. Averroës drew another sharp distinction between soul and intellect, the latter being of a superior kind if only because of its absolute freedom from matter.

Culminating in Averroës, Arab philosophy bore fruit in the intellectual and rational trends of subsequent centuries. Within the confines of his philosophical knowledge, Averroës discovered a measure of certitude which informed his epochal reply to al-Ghazzali. The basic conception to which he appealed was that the noble does not exist by virtue of the less noble but vice versa.

This Arab philosophy reached the Latin West through diverse channels, primary among which was the Hebrew. When Archdeacon Gundisalvus of Seville was commissioned in the early twelfth century by Raymond, archbishop of Toledo, to make translations of Avicenna, he was assisted by Avendeath (c. 1090–1165), a convert from Judaism. Their translation of Avicenna's *On the Soul* — a commentary on Aristotle's great treatise — exercised considerable influence on the West. Maimonides (1135–1204) formulated the evidence for the existence, unity, and incorporeality of God with the aid of Aristotelian metaphysics embedded in Avicenna's writings; his attack on the Mutakallimun was freely utilized by Thomas Aquinas (1227–1274).

Intent upon saving both the Platonist immortality of the soul and the Aristotelian unity of the human composite, Christian philosophers were naturally drawn to Avicenna. They recognized in him those elements of Platonism which were already incorporated in their tradition since Saint Augustine. Precisely this, together with those Aristotelian concepts which Christians were able to accept, occasioned the influx of Arab philosophy into Western theology. The trend was unmistakable: Avicenna was accepted after an attempt was made to rid him of uncongenial views, and, having reduced his principles to agree with Saint Augustine, it was possible to admit his interpretations as part of a necessary Aristotelianism.

LITERATURE

Arabic literature is largely the product of Islamic culture. It drew upon the gifts of many races in different lands, yet remained essentially Semitic in form, continuing to some degree the Hebrew, Aramaic, and kindred heritages. A luxuriant literary growth, it falls into the departments of religious and secular writings. One of the salient features of this literary development is an ancient attachment to poetry balanced by an esteem for the prose of the Koran. An excessive rigidity of literary criticism tended to promote the sacrifice of substance for form. Whereas religion, science, history, biography, geography, philosophy, and rhetoric determined the medieval literary scene, today politics, social concern, foreign affairs, journalism, and a popular press are in the ascendancy.

Since the latter part of the nineteenth century, the advent of the Arabic theater has produced a harvest of dramas and novels, and given birth to the modern story and play. It is a question, however, whether Arabic style has as yet fully adjusted to the shift from handwriting to the printing press. Translations from foreign languages do not at present match in selectivity — though they outstrip in volume — those of medieval times. *The Arabian Nights* may be said to portray the popular and universal genius of traditional Arabic literature.

In its broad sweep, Arabic literature breathes the spirit of verbal and aesthetic rather than technical and scientific perception. This literary lag is partly due to the general apathy inherited from centuries of foreign rule.

Surely the classic theory of this literature lends itself admirably as a forceful vehicle for democratic ideals. Yet despite the Western impact, modern creativity has not fully caught up with the true spirit of twentieth century freedom. An intimation of a revival might be seen in the greater balance struck between the regional and the particular, the local and the universal themes. As a force behind the Islamic cultural pattern, this literature has great significance. Through it, the best minds react and interact upon each other. Through the reading and production of books and articles on science, history, politics, philosophy, and so forth, the Middle East critically examines and re-examines its own nature and destiny.

Whether in the Middle East, Pakistan, or elsewhere in the world-wide Islamic community, culture rests upon a common ground of religious and historic traditions. The first spark that ignited this cultural system was undoubtedly religious in origin, and its fuller development cannot be divorced from religious premises. But the particular literature that best reveals the essence of Islamic civilization sprang from both allegiance to the Koran and reproduction in daily life of a pre-Islamic spirit transmitted in poetry and prose.

Beyond the Koran and the other literary documents that came into being, moreover, were other streams that fed the ever-widening river of medieval Islam. These were streams flowing out of Persia and Greece. From Greece came orderly thought, philosophy, science, and psychological gifts. From Persia came artistry, mystical strains, epic and dramatic themes which in due course encouraged and enriched literary productivity. But the central motif of Islamic literature, in its lyrical, autobiographical, and dogmatic character, was fundamentally Arab in inspiration.

The basic assumption of literary theory among the Arabs was inherent in the belief that self-expression through words, spoken or written, was the highest artistic form open to mankind. The art of speech as such was therefore conceived as the chief vehicle of culture and refinement. It surpassed in value every conceivable achievement in the realm of music and sculpture, which with all their splendor must remain insufficient and vague compared with the eloquence and brilliance of verbal expression.

The Arabic word for literature is *adab,* implying the sense of *da'b,* that is, steady work and perseverance. But the word meant infinitely more. It really connoted the noble and humane faculties of the human soul and their exercise in the conduct of life and social intercourse. Equally arresting are those definitions that make artistic expression " equal to two thirds of religion," or that esteem the knowledge of literature as a process leading to an intellectual culture of a higher degree and making possible a more refined social development of the individual as a result of training in philology, poetry, exegesis, and ancient history.

Such a glorification of verbal expression is the hallmark of Islamic civilization. It is the key to the literary genius of the Middle East. It is the most obvious element in the culture of the Arabs, who created alongside the Byzantine and Latin worlds a world of their own excelling the other two in vitality and intellectual refinement.

The aspects of science, philosophy, and literature which our study of Islamic culture brought out are of more than passing interest. Such background information might conceivably lead to sounder judgment on the predicament and opportunity of the Middle East. A revolution in the region's cultural and intellectual life could come if critical study of philosophers such as Avicenna and Averroës were seriously embarked upon.

9

MIDDLE EAST AND WORLD PEACE

I T IS common knowledge that the three monotheistic religions originating in the Middle East share a historic kinship
and intimacy. Their obvious disparities and discords notwithstanding, they rightly claim a number of highly significant
similarities. The story that largely remains untold, however, is
how Islam, Christianity, and Judaism once acted in unison. Not
infrequently they released creative powers of cohesion in the
world round about.

That this potential of good will can be released again, even
more forcefully, in our own age, is a top secret about which little is said and much less written or done. Yet, if courageously
approached, and imaginatively utilized, this spiritual resource
may well tip the scales in favor of peace within the region.
That is the kind of peace that in due course might contribute
toward the establishment of a more stable international order.

Thrilling and humbling is the vision that arises. For as we
contemplate these three major religions, noting their common
ground as well as their feuds and rifts, thoughts of human solidarity and reconciliation in the vast domains that spread before us are inspired. To think of Middle East Islam is soon to
be confronted with a world-wide Islamic community of over
three hundred million souls. As for the Christianity which began when the tiny community of Jesus' followers in Antioch
came to be known as Christians, today it envelops the inhabited world. The total of Eastern Orthodox, Roman Catholic,

Protestant, and other Christians nearly strikes the eight hundred million mark. The very thought of the region's Judaism, moreover, conjures up the spectacle of a cosmopolitan Jewry influential in foreign affairs; it is a community dynamic in human progress along the cultural, technical, and economic fronts.

Now consider seriously the question as to what the Middle East would be like, indeed what the entire world might gain, if the adherents of these three venerable faiths were to walk shoulder to shoulder; what, if they determined to explore whatever pertains to the unity and welfare of their common homelands and the world. Lest anyone suspect that the above idea is merely the product of academic speculation, we make bold to affirm that the incentive to work together is implicit in the ancient bond that draws Islam, Christianity, and Judaism to each other.

Such a partnership derives its hard core from a common ground. It may be sketched under the three heads of the phenomena of religion, of order and organization, and of an ultimate reality. All these factors bring the three religions into close proximity.

PHENOMENA OF RELIGION

That the three systems of religious experience under investigation have been creative of culture is a fact that validates their community of interest in the modern world. This is in keeping with the verdict that religion is not merely useful for guidance and inspiration of civilization but the very reason for its existence.

Thus the Islamic religious movement which overran the countries extending from Arabia westward to Spain, and from Baghdad into India and beyond, was the prelude to a far-flung empire of the mind and spirit. And who can explain without Christianity that mighty wave of culture emergent in the ancient Orient and Greece? Spreading out, it entrenched itself on the continent of Europe, then many centuries after crossed the

Atlantic. It rose in time to challenging heights of technical and intellectual creativity. Judaism likewise has reared a perennial culture to which other civilizations are under heavy debt.

Nowhere is this creativity more striking than in the incentive it gave the production of classical writing. Take, for example, that technical and impressively mature literature which in its medieval effervescence Islam promoted. It is moreover true that whether they evolved in monastery or laboratory, Western learning and science owed Christian initiative something; although European colleges and universities for the most part had an independent growth, they as well as the very inception of American scholarship were under Christian influence. Operating often under distressing conditions, Judaism likewise fostered in Talmudic academy and rabbinical studium a passion for learning. Hence the vast treasures of wisdom and philosophical thought for which Spain and Sicily, as Palestine, Babylon, and Egypt earlier, provided the setting.

A serious issue in varying degrees haunting the three faiths revolved on the tension between their theocratic propositions and the requirements of an ever-expanding secular order. Since the Reformation, the West has resolved the problem here encountered through a series of adjustments under the rather ambiguous rubric of separation between Church and State. Although much solid thinking remains to be done in this crucial area, yet the amazing receptivity of the three religious communities to what is involved is further evidence of a similarity in outlook on juridical, political, and constitutional matters. Closely related are the problems of international relations and human rights, where the Biblical and Koranic injunctions provide the grounds for reinterpretation and deduction from first principles.

Thus the three religions across history grappled with new human situations, creating institutions and forming traditions. Today they are faced with the most fateful challenge of all. It is to accept the principle of coexistence not only among nations but among the great religions as well, as a framework endorsed by faith, supported by reason, and deemed conducive to peace.

Supremely, under this caption of religious phenomena, the three religions — despite rigidity of outlook and the temptation to become ingrown — evolved a high elasticity. They cultivated the kind of live-and-let-live outlook which, more than a mere device, had deep roots in their basic structures. And strangely enough, exclusiveness often generated its direct opposite. A humane and inclusive trait reconciled to the existence of others was calculated to balance off dogmatic separation by an openness of mind and a genuine desire to give and take.

All of which was of course true to the exalted affirmations of the faiths concerned. Despite emphasis on holy war and the ostensible reproach of other systems, Islam did not fail to heed the Koranic dictum: " Lo! those who believe (in that which is revealed to thee, Muhammad), and those who are Jews and Christians, and Sabaeans — whoever believeth in God and the Last Day and doeth right — surely their reward is with their Lord, and there shall no fear come upon them, neither shall they grieve " (2:59).

Inherent in Christianity, furthermore, is a love for those outside, the enemy and alien. In the parable of the Good Samaritan (Luke 10:30–37), and elsewhere, Jesus lifted to an enviable position those capable of the kind of neighborliness that each of us needs to emulate. Judaism conceived of an acceptable order for the Gentiles; for them, the laws of Noah served a high purpose and were actually as valid as the law of Moses was for the Hebrews. And who can ignore the words of Isaiah (ch. 19:25) which, transcending Israel's enmity and strife with its giant neighbors, declared: " Blessed be Egypt my people, and Assyria the work of my hands, and Israel my heritage "?

ORDER AND ORGANIZATION

Another principal similarity hinges on the fact that in the three religions a specialized personnel is vested with responsibility consequent to careful recruitment and vigorous training. Whether essentially learned, hierarchical, or Levitical; whether ministerial, rabbinical, or Azharite; in the authority to teach, preach, and officiate at worship services, the three religions bestow privilege upon and attach prestige to the religious offices.

Someone might object that Islam is strictly nonecclesiastical at the core. To this we should hasten to reply that cadis, muftis, sheiks, imams, and the class of ulema generally do perform duties analogous with those of rabbi, priest, and clergyman. Their role in society and impact upon the community make for order and organization.

Steeped in scholarship, members of this specialized personnel down the ages have produced classics sensitive to the issues that agitate the mind and alive to the contemporary scene. Professor Harry Austryn Wolfson of Harvard composed a monumental work on the Hellenistic-Jewish philosopher Philo (c. 20 B.C.–A.D. 54). A sunrise figure, his contribution presumably set the pace for some of the profound aspects of religious thought in Judaism, Islam, and Christianity. Augustine and Thomas Aquinas in Christianity, al-Ghazzali and Muhammad Abduh in Islam, Maimonides and Martin Buber in Judaism — to single out a few at random — were thinkers who saw revealed truth and the findings of reason in a unity of compelling radiance.

The authority of a sacred Book, interpreted by devout and versatile men, imparted to these religions an aura of plausibility. Translated into order and organization, this made for reliability. It created in the believer both intellectual precision and honesty as in obedience of faith he followed the dictates of conscience and sought to live by the truth that makes free.

Hence the emergence of an integrating principle and the establishment of corporate bodies of believers did not proceed merely from the will of rulers. Nor did it solely rest upon the designs of those who exercised dictatorial control. Seen in the light of history's long-range perspective, order and organization were an abiding testimony to that resilience and prudence whereby the truth was communicated and incarnated in constructive undertakings.

What reason and the appeal to the intellect and spirit did to render religious authority more tenable, the cults and rituals accomplished in behalf of the common man. The Sabbath, Sunday, Friday, and sundry festivals and holidays meant relaxation and exaltation. In a manner distinctively their own, the religions before us provided for the individual and community the means to practice the presence of God. Worship was not exhausted, however, by ritual, since the dimension of converse with God had of necessity to be safeguarded.

This open door to the Eternal gave rise to three parallel manifestations of mysticism. In the realm of art and architecture, it gave rise to a world-wide distribution of synagogues and cathedrals, mosques, churches, and shrines where order and organization came to a visible focus.

Ultimate Reality

Beyond the phenomena of religion and transcending order and organization, the kinship of Islam, Christianity, and Judaism extends to the deeper level of things ultimate, where the final objectives of being are encountered. The Divine Being is adored not simply in acts and performances subject to given forms of government, but, what is infinitely more significant, in creeds, confessions, and dogmatic formulations that enshrine the faith and crystallize the doctrine.

The belief that there is one God, eternal, sovereign, righteous, and compassionate, informs the whole structure of theistic faith. That religion is essentially revealed truth is another pivotal point in the tradition common to the three faiths. Further identity of design arises where luminous figures such as Enoch, Noah, Abraham, Isaac, Jacob, Job, and Jonah, as well as certain prophets and a group of sacred documents, are uniformly accepted by all. Each community, in a manner strictly its own, regards itself the society of destiny, the people of a Book, be it Torah, Bible, or Koran.

Equally unifying as a principle is the conception of man, created by God and made the object of individual love and providence, the recipient of divine grace, imbued with dignity, freedom, and immortality. For his earthly enlightenment and guidance, divine law was instituted, a law that will transform the wilderness of nature into a veritable abode of peace.

Quite as striking a sign of uniformity is discovered in the philosophy of history that is shared. History is conceived as subject to the Eternal's decrees, and, having a beginning as well as a final fulfillment, it is eminently meaningful. The concept of divine purpose has bequeathed to Moslems, Christians, and Jews a deathless hope that the righteous God who can do no evil will not abandon his people; that despite man's folly and the tragedy of our existence, he will carry out his promises and blessings unto a wise and absolutely just consummation.

Fortified by so profound a vision and grounded in the faith that a righteous Eternal presides over human destiny, believers of these three religions have generally conceived of the whole world as their household and regarded mankind as their parish. In different ways, therefore, they have aspired to diffuse knowledge of the Eternal, to propagate the faith, and to lead the human procession in its advance toward peace and the true religion.

In the exercise of that singular responsibility, the three religions have sought to win the world to their doctrines and ways of life. Whether in the preaching of Islam and the expansion of Koranic faith in Allah, in Christian missions, or in the intellectual and scholarly initiative of Judaism, the world stood greatly in awe as it learned more about an Eternal who is merciful and redeeming. Yet we must never delude ourselves into thinking that the so-called nontheists of the race were completely denied all knowledge of the supreme Lord. Indeed the universality of the knowledge of God is a theme underscored by Christianity itself under the article of general revelation.

Surely, the most pressing concern of our time is that of war and peace. Here followers of the sister faiths, as they consolidate their efforts and brace themselves for the spiritual struggle against tyranny, need to draw upon their ultimate resource, which is eternal truth. In heart-searching dedication they must order their lives and prepare for the choice between good and evil, the hinge of destiny upon which victory through defeat must in the end depend. The answer to the world's agony must inevitably come in terms of an Eternal who will not let his people perish.

We have seen how this area of agreement extends to the very threshold of ultimacy and sheds light upon the meaning of time and eternity. Do not all three religions rest the case for a hereafter upon the nature of God — Creator, Lord of Life — who will not leave man in the dust?

But eternity itself is not related to time in the form of a straight line connecting this life and the next. Eternity is another unique dimension of upright living and vision which intersects this temporal existence. To live in eternity is to live a life of faith, vision, and brotherly love both now and forever.

The glory of the view upheld by all three faiths is that history is a meaningful drama. And this involves us all in the responsibility of coming to terms with the temporal world, that is, with man, nature, and society, so that, loving each other in faith and in truth — as Christians, Moslems, and Jews — we might together build a better world.

The Great Religions and World Peace

Although scarcely more than an illusion thus far, world peace and the hope for a secure international structure form a deathless vision. This hope and vision spring eternal, deriving their perennial scope and character from the human depths, their essence from religious faith and pure reason. In our own day, the hope for peace sets for the great religions of the modern world a quest for common understanding and partnership in certain given areas of communal and foreign affairs. This may be said to parallel that other kindred quest within the secular and political order which finds its noblest expression in the creation and maintenance of the United Nations.

The problem of peace is, to be sure, as old as it is abstruse;

nor is there any great novelty about the claim that its ultimate resolution — if it ever comes — will hinge entirely or in part upon the things of the spirit and be interlocked with the interfaith pattern.

Yet the fact that in the international sphere we have already moved into a new orbit — for which coexistence is apparently the correct keyword — imposes upon those who take the field of comparative religion seriously a grave responsibility to initiate the kind of creative intellectual leadership that might be commensurate with the challenging opportunity that comes with the coexistence not only of conflicting political ideologies but of religions as well.

Trygve Lie's memoirs, *In the Cause of Peace,* convey the distinct impression that the world organization which he served as first Secretary-General in the seven formative years 1946–1953, might quite conceivably stand more erect and become significantly less ineffective were the tremendous prestige of the great religions thrown solidly behind it. It ought to make a startling difference if, among the world's populations of diverse creeds, the authority and wills of the living religions were consistently and decisively felt on the side of peace. Nor can such a powerful current of religious enthusiasm long fail to induce response in the councils of the nations.

If and when the living religions decide to speak in unison, the major issues of our time will be sharpened. These are fundamentally four in number. In organizing their vast intercultural and interreligious potential against tyranny, Islam, Christianity, and Judaism are bound to confront the following primary concerns of mankind.

First, there is the global-anthropological issue. Although the systematic annihilation of time and space has outwardly created of the whole world a single community, yet it has failed to transform the earth into anything like a neighborhood. Secondly, there is the issue of diplomacy and international affairs. The four basic facts here are: the United States of America as a first-rate power; the emergence of Marxist ideology and its entrenchment at the heart of the Russian empire; the retreat of Europe from its former ascendancy; and the release on the continent of Asia of a long dormant dynamism. Third is the issue of culture. The priority attached to materialism threatens to dislodge Western man from his ancient moorings; the centrality of technocracy produces a decadence which spells out the diminution of interest in pure thought with its twin attributes of faith and reason. Fourthly, in the realm of metaphysics proper as well as in philosophy, the issue may be stated in terms of the heightened significance of the ultimately real. This is brought home in the dilemma between good and evil, war and peace, ethics and expediency, ways and means, truth and falsehood, as well as in confrontation with the perennial questions with regard to life and death, being and nonbeing, destiny, love, order, freedom, and justice.

Freedom in the Truth

Three religions — Islam, Buddhism, and Christianity — claim universality in the modern world, and majorities of their adherents are paramount, respectively, in the Middle East, in Asia, and in the West.

At their deepest level, both Islam and Buddhism display validity and vitality which account for their spontaneous appeal and do not altogether contradict the unique and distinctive character of Christianity. In upholding the doctrines of freedom in the truth, we ought to press for a greater degree of understanding and freer intercourse among the followers of these three faiths. Let us be confident in the belief that the truth is its own best apologetic and that it will inevitably vindicate itself and triumph in the end.

The greatness of Islam and the genius of its universality and popularity rest in the proclamation that God is, that he is one, eternal, almighty, sovereign, self-revealing, and arbitrer of ends. There can be no possible reproach of Islam on those grounds. In so far as that glorious affirmation goes, Christians can have no quarrel with Moslems.

Christianity finds the truth in the person of Jesus Christ. He reveals the truth about God, that he is love, and about man, that he is a sinner who can be redeemed. Christ is the author and finisher of Christian faith, since in him the grace of God shone forth, calling the sinner to penitence and in forgiveness providing the beginning of a new life of commitment and joy. Although different in essence, and penetrating beyond either Islam or Buddhism, Christianity need not repudiate the elements of truth and spirituality in those religions.

The veritable Western tradition, founded on revealed Biblical truth — voiced by the Hebrew prophets and climaxed in the person and gospel of the Redeemer — emerged as a living communication when it had emanated through the reason and studied accuracy bequeathed by the Greek mind and spirit. This living communication was in turn assimilated by Europe and bore that continent's testimony enshrined in an incomparable literature and transmitted in works of art, as well as in the classics written by saint, scholar, and philosopher.

Such a fundamental concern with the things of the spirit — fortified by philosophy and experience — became the object of life and imbued thought with meaning. It absorbed and coordinated whatever germinal truth was to be garnered elsewhere, and thus stemmed the tide of decadence. In essence, decadence may be defined as an idolatry that sets the clock of progress — growth in grace — back toward the deification of nature, man, matter, or the cosmos.

The above interpretation of the Western tradition at its best permits the treatment of some of the conspicuous movements of our time as a retreat from the exalted vision of the West. Nationalism, Communism, and militant Zionism — to single out three defections — may be brought under control if the spirit of the West, rightly so-called, is positively affirmed. Thus nationalism, setting up its tribal gods; Communism, declaring the ultimacy of matter; and militant Zionism, contravening the mystery of Israel by an idolatry of land and people, must all be made subject to a catharsis that rejects the idols and refuses to identify the Absolute and Eternal with any of the hollow earth gods.

In *Ambassador's Report,* Chester Bowles said, "I believe that the history of our time will hereafter be written in Asia." The sooner we recognize that those with whom we disagree in Asia have something to say, and the more our idealism is tempered with a realism that does not expect too much from men and politics, the happier in the end will be our relations with the peoples of a continent which is the mother of all races.

THE INEVITABILITY OF ARTICULATION

Until they articulate on the frontiers of existence, both knowledge and truth remain irrelevant, and religion in that case is reduced to the category of frozen dogma. That it may be effectively articulate, a given religion must make foreign affairs, diplomacy, culture, economics, and education its natural frontiers. Either its truth becomes meaningful and vibrant within the contexts of these and other fields of modern life, or religion loses the battle by default.

To live in a state of friendly yet fierce tension with other religions is the supreme challenge that comes to every living faith. Such is the determination that creative religion has bequeathed to education and that education at its best ordains for itself. An illustrious educator — President Harold W. Dodds of Princeton — had this to say at a conference in 1954, when Columbia University celebrated its bicentennial: "What we call a university, both in its medieval origin and as we know it today, with all its modern and often dismaying complexity, is the institution which the Western world has established for realizing man's right to knowledge and the free use thereof." With academic freedom in mind, Dr. Dodds maintained that the university remains our one great instrumentality for discovering and sharing the truth. He observed, however, that it is difficult for the public to grasp the idea that a university exists for the purpose of entertaining, even generating, differences of opinion, rather than achieving uniformity of outlook.

For a religious group to shrink back from an orderly and open-minded debate with the followers of other faiths is to sign the death warrant of its own creed. No religion can any longer claim the right to absolute veracity while it lives in splendid isolation.

Invaluable contributions toward the establishment of a world community are in sight. Articulate and deliberate vitalization of our interest in the great religions may provide the solution to any number of the ills that presently afflict the divided human society. Some of the benefits that are in store may be touched upon.

1. Promotion of the understanding of religion and a heightened grasp of one's own faith at its best.

2. Provision of an effective expression of the universal human longing for a world in which estranged communities can become one in sharing their different spiritual dynamisms.

3. With accent upon religion as the core of culture, the fellowship and neighborliness of all peoples, rather than their grievances and feuds, will be brought to the foreground.

4. Thus to seek the truth provides on a high level the right climate for the pursuit of such common interests as might produce the desired goals of peace and security.

To own reverence for the best in the cultures and religious traditions of others — an old Middle East tradition — is to promote the cause of world peace.

In the book of Genesis we read of Noah's experiment in farming and his experience with wine. The sorry scene of the aged man's nakedness is relieved at last by the intervention of his two sons, Shem and Japheth. They walk up to their intoxicated father and throw the garment of decency about his sprawled out and naked body. Something of the true Middle East comes alive in that ancient parable.

A similar vein of understanding, I trust, runs through this book. Middle East and world peace have been an ever-present concern. Four vital themes constantly came to mind. These are the Arab-Islamic drama, the Judaeo-Christian frame of reference, America's responsibility, and the implications of the East-West conflict.

Granted perseverance and wisdom, followers of the three great faiths who are possessed of the truth shall yet ascend together the summit of peace. That ascent begins as relations with the United States are improved and regional strains are relieved.

SUGGESTED READINGS

Confined to books and journals conveniently available in English, this supplemental list does not reproduce titles already cited in the main text.

I. The United States and the Middle East

Halford S. Hoskins, *Middle East: Problem Area in World Politics.* The Macmillan Company, 1954.

J. C. Hurewitz, *Middle East Dilemmas: The Background of United States Policy.* Harper & Brothers, 1953.

George Kirk, *The Middle East in the War.* Oxford University Press, London, 1953.

Hans Kohn, *A History of Nationalism in the East.* Harcourt, Brace and Company, Inc., 1929.

Reinhold Niebuhr, *The Irony of American History.* Charles Scribner's Sons, 1952.

Stephen B. L. Penrose, Jr., *That They May Have Life.* Trustees of American University of Beirut, New York, 1941.

E. A. Speiser, *The United States and the Near East.* Harvard University Press, 1951.

L. V. Thomas and R. N. Frye, *The United States and Turkey and Iran.* Harvard University Press, 1951.

II. Inside the Middle East

N. S. Fatemi, *Oil Diplomacy.* Whittier Books, Inc., 1954.

W. B. Fisher, *The Middle East: A Physical, Social, and Regional Geography.* E. P. Dutton & Co., Inc., 1950.

R. N. Frye, Editor, *The Near East and the Great Powers.* Harvard University Press, 1951.

Harvey P. Hall, Editor, *The Evolution of Public Responsibility in*

156

the Middle East. Middle East Institute, Washington, D.C., 1955.

Ralph Linton, Editor, *Most of the World.* Columbia University Press, 1949.

S. H. Longrigg, *Oil in the Middle East.* Oxford University Press, London, 1954.

The Middle East Journal. Middle East Institute, Washington, D.C.

III. Islam: A Religious Tradition

A. J. Arberry, *The Korán Interpreted,* 2 vols. The Macmillan Company, 1955.

Carl Brockelmann, *History of the Islamic Peoples.* G. P. Putnam's Sons, 1947.

H. G. Dorman, Jr., *Toward Understanding Islam.* Teachers College, Columbia University, 1948.

H. A. R. Gibb, *Mohemmedanism.* Oxford University Press, London, 1949.

Alfred Guillaume, *Islam.* Penguin Books, 1954.

Philip K. Hitti, *History of the Arabs.* The Macmillan Company, London, 1940.

Majid Khadduri and H. J. Liebesny, *Law in the Middle East.* Middle East Institute, Washington, D.C., 1955.

IV. The Eastern Churches: Origins

A. Alföldi, *The Conversion of Constantine and Pagan Rome.* Oxford University Press, 1948.

A. Harnack, *The Expansion of Christianity in the First Three Centuries.* Williams & Norgate, Ltd., London, 1905.

Ernest Jackh, Editor, *Background of the Middle East.* Cornell University Press, 1952.

K. S. Latourette, *A History of the Expansion of Christianity,* Vol. I, *The First Five Centuries.* Harper & Brothers, 1937.

A. P. Stanley, *Lectures on the History of the Eastern Church.* Charles Scribner's Sons, 1907.

V. Four Christian Traditions

Sarkis Atamian, *The Armenian Community.* Philosophical Library, 1955.

Donald Attwater, *The Dissident Eastern Churches.* Bruce Publishing Company, 1937.

E. R. Hardy, *Christian Egypt: Church and People.* Oxford University Press, New York, 1952.

P. K. Hitti, *History of Syria.* The Macmillan Company, 1951.

A. H. Hourani, *Minorities in the Arab World*. Royal Institute of International Affairs, London, 1947.

K. S. Latourette, *A History of Christianity*. Harper & Brothers, 1953.

W. A. Wigram, *An Introduction to the History of the Assyrian Church or the Church of the Sassanian Persian Empire, 100–640* A.D. Society for Promoting Christian Knowledge, London, 1910.

VI. RECORD OF JUDAISM

David Ben-Gurion, *Rebirth and Destiny of Israel*. Philosophical Library, 1954.

Norman Bentwich, *For Zion's Sake: A Biography of Judah L. Magnes*. The Jewish Publication Society of America, 1954.

Elmer Berger, *Who Knows Better Must Say So!* American Council for Judiasm, 1955.

Martin Buber, *Israel and the World*. Schocken Books, Inc., 1948.

S. D. Goitein, *Jews and Arabs: Their Contacts Through the Ages*. Schocken Books, Inc., 1955.

Alfred M. Lilienthal, *What Price Israel?* Henry Regnery Co., 1953.

Raphael Patai, *Israel Between East and West*. The Jewish Publication Society of America, 1953.

VII. IMPACT OF PROTESTANT CHRISTIANITY

A Century of Mission Work in Iran (Persia), 1834–1934. American Press, Beirut (no date or author).

Henry Harris Jessup, *Fifty-three Years in Syria*, 2 vols. Fleming H. Revell Co., 1910.

The International Review of Missions. International Missionary Council, London.

The Muslin World, a quarterly journal. Hartford Seminary Foundation, Hartford, Conn.

Julius Richter, *A History of Protestant Missions in the Near East*. Oliphant, Anderson, and Ferrier, Edinburgh, 1910.

P. E. Shaw, *American Contacts with the Eastern Churches, 1820–1870*. American Society for Church History, 1937.

VIII. AN ISLAMIC CULTURAL PATTERN

N. A. Faris, Editor, *The Arab Heritage*. Princeton University Press, 1944.

N. A. Faris and M. T. Husayn, *The Crescent in Crisis*. University of Kansas Press, 1955.

F. W. Fernau, *Moslems on the March*. Alfred A. Knopf, Inc., 1954.

S. N. Fisher, Editor, *Social Forces in the Middle East*. Cornell University Press, 1955.

G. E. Von Grunebaum, *Medieval Islam.* University of Chicago Press, 1946.

T. Cuyler Young, Editor, *Near Eastern Culture and Society.* Princeton University Press, 1951.

IX. MIDDLE EAST AND WORLD PEACE

P. H. Ashby, *The Conflict of Religions.* Charles Scribner's Sons, 1955.

John Baillie, *The Belief in Progress.* Charles Scribner's Sons, 1951.

Herbert Butterfield, *Christianity, Diplomacy, and War.* Abingdon Press, n. d.

E. C. Dewick, *The Christian Attitude to Other Religions.* Cambridge University Press, 1953.

W. E. Hocking, *Living Religions and a World Faith.* The Macmillan Company, 1934.

G. M. Kahin, *The Asian-African Conference, Bandung, Indonesia.* Cornell University Press, 1956.

W. C. Lamott, *Revolution in Missions.* The Macmillan Company, 1954.

K. S. Latourette, *Challenge and Conformity.* Harper & Brothers, 1955.

A. William Loos, Editor, *Religious Faith and World Culture.* Prentice-Hall, Inc., 1951.

Paul Tillich, *Love, Power, and Justice.* Oxford University Press, New York, 1954.

Arnold Toynbee, *The World and the West.* Oxford University Press, New York, 1953.